Business Communication:
A Classroom Simulation

James B. Stull, Ph.D.
John W. Baird, Ph.D.

College of Business
San Jose State University

Prentice Hall Career & Technology, Englewood Cliffs, New Jersey 07632

Library of Congress Cataloging-in-Publication Data
Stull, James.
   Business communication : a classroom simulation / James B. Stull ,
John W. Baird.
      p.   cm.
   Includes index.
   ISBN 0-13-092503-9
   1. Business communication--Simulation methods.   I. Baird, John
William, 1944 -   .   II. Title.
HF 5718.S84   1993
658.4'5--dc20

                                                    92 - 14971
                                                    CIP

Editorial/production supervision : *Marcia Krefetz*
Cover design: *Bruce Kenselaar*
Prepress buyer: *Ilene Levy*
Manufacturing buyer: *Ed O'Dougherty*
Acquisitions editor: *Elizabeth Sugg*

 © 1993 by Prentice Hall Career & Technology
Prentice-Hall, Inc.
A Paramount Communications Company
Englewood Cliffs, New Jersey 07632

Printed in the United States of America

10 9 8 7 6 5 4

ISBN   0-13-092503-9

PRENTICE-HALL INTERNATIONAL (UK) LIMITED, London
PRENTICE-HALL OF AUSTRALIA PTY. LIMITED, Sydney
PRENTICE-HALL CANADA INC., Toronto
PRENTICE-HALL HISPANOAMERICANA, S.A., Mexico
PRENTICE-HALL OF INDIA PRIVATE LIMITED, New Delhi
PRENTICE-HALL OF JAPAN, INC., Tokyo
SIMON & SCHUSTER ASIA PTE. LTD., Singapore
EDITORA PRENTICE-HALL DO BRASIL, LTDA., Rio de Janeiro

CONTENTS

PREFACE

During the fall semester of 1987, the two of us authors were talking one morning about the need to add new excitement to our business communication classes. For a few years we had talked about developing a simulation that would allow students to assume organizational roles in their own companies and interact with each other about business issues. Since we were team teaching a section of the course, we decided that the time was "now" to develop and begin running the simulation. We were already two or three weeks into the semester. At the next class meeting, we introduced our students to what we had been able to create in two days.

Our students were cooperative and excited about experimenting in the classroom. We stumbled through some things, sailed through others, and ended the semester having "created as we went" the beginnings of the simulation presented in this book. Having successfully used this simulation for several semesters, we have worked out most of the bugs.

Students tell us the simulation is a great way to learn about business communication. They consistently report that the simulation is "like the real world," dealing with current events and real people. The class earns praise t as exciting, stimulating and a great contrast to most of their other academic experiences. Students claim that they learn more and that they enjoy coming to class.

In 1988, we presented a paper on the simulation to members of the Association for Business Communication, and received enthusiastic encouragement from faculty and textbook representatives to publish it in book form. Two colleagues offered to use the simulation in their classrooms: We thank Professor Judy Lease, University of Utah, for experimenting with it when she was at Tulane University; and Dr. Karon Cunningham, Southwest Missouri State University, for using it when she was at West Texas State University. One of our concerns was that our Silicon Valley theme would not apply to other areas where the course is taught. Feedback from Texas and Louisiana indicated that students there adapt easily to the "high-tech" scenario and still find the simulation to be very real.

Simulating conditions that people can expect to face in their careers is a popular and practical way to learn and to develop skills. Participants can gain many of the benefits of real-world experiences without having to pay real-world prices for their mistakes. The classroom laboratory is typically a safe environment for experimentation.

This book is unique: It differs from all other traditional business communication books because it is organized around the simulation. Rather than consisting of a series of disconnected exercises and mini-simulations, *Business Communication: A Classroom Simulation* integrates an entire semester's material into one overall scheme in which you use communication to attempt to resolve business issues. When planning and creating your messages, you need to be aware of your company's culture, your role within that company, and your professional and interpersonal relationships with the classmates with whom you will be interacting.

The simulation is divided into six units. *Unit 1, Communication in Organizations: Getting Back to Basics*, briefly presents the communication process and then covers the fundamentals of business writing, Seven C's: clarity, completeness, conciseness, coherence, correctness, concreteness, and courtesy. Numerous examples and exercises are presented. Your instructor may elect to complete this unit before embarking on the simulation. If he or she does not, you may be encouraged to return to this unit when you need additional assistance with some of these basic concepts. We like to present certain topics in the form of executive seminars or workshops, much like a corporate training program.

In *Unit 2, Introduction to the Simulation: Developing Corporate Culture*, you will form your company, decide who will play which roles, learn more about your own role, learn about your company's history and culture, add more information to your corporate culture, design a letterhead and a logo, write letters of introduction to your counterparts in the other companies, create a brochure or corporate culture statement that your team will distribute to each participant in the simulation, and unveil your company to the other companies at the Silicon Valley Fair.

Unit 3, Employment Communications Writing Messages that Get the Job, presents ideas and exercises for writing effective résumés, cover letters, and follow-up messages. It also includes information on employment interviews, presenting questions and exercises from the perspectives of both the interviewer and the interviewee. You will actually tailor your own résumé and cover letter to a position created and posted by members of one of the other simulation companies. You will also have the opportunity to interview other classmates and to be interviewed by them. At the end of this unit, you will evaluate and report on the résumés, cover letters, and interviews, and you will let the class know who you would actually hire.

Unit 4, Routine and Good News Messages: Using the Direct Approach, provides a simple model and numerous examples of how to write direct messages. Most business messages are routine and some are actually good news. These can typically be presented directly, without any need for special treatment. Thirty different problems are included at the end of this unit. Most of them are based on current business events presented in *The Wall Street Journal* and other sources. You will be assigned one or more problems during this unit that will require that you write to your counterpart(s) in one or more of the other companies. Remember to present the main idea first, and you will find the unit to be straightforward.

Unit 5, Negative and Persuasive Messages: Using the Indirect Approach, presents a model and examples of how to write indirect messages. Bad news and negative messages often require an indirect approach by which you prepare your reader for your main point before actually delivering it. Then you try to get him or her to accept your decision. Persuasive messages, too, typically follow the indirect approach. You may need to show the other person the benefits of your appeal before asking that person for any commitment. Thirty different problems have been created for this unit, mostly based on current issues found in the business sections of major newspapers. During this unit, you will be assigned one or more problems that will require that you write to your counterpart(s) in one or more of the other companies. Flexibility and creativity may be appropriate in dealing with some of the problems. The important thing is to know how to be indirect when you need to be.

In *Unit 6, Business Proposals: Writing More Detailed Messages*, you and your team will write and present a proposal to one of the other companies. You will be asked to research a topic of your choice, organize it into a persuasive written business proposal, and present it in a business meeting to the executive committee of another company. You will learn to write a concise problem statement that keeps you on track throughout the experience. You will develop, modify, and follow an outline that best presents your ideas in the most logical, persuasive manner. You will have an opportunity to be creative in both written and oral expression, within reason and good taste.

During each unit, you are encouraged to complete *self-initiated assignments* (SIAs). In many of your classes you respond to assignments that are given by your instructor or found in textbooks. Usually, you are given a certain amount of information and you work within the constraints of the problem. Sometimes, however, you just decide to do something: "I think I'll write a letter to Carla [Bob, Professor Wong, Senator Green, etc.]." In business, you must often *initiate* messages or you may *elect to respond* to messages that you receive. In this simulation you are encouraged or may be required to initiate a number of messages on your own. You will have more choice about the content.

The simulation has been designed to be modified to fit a particular teaching style. *Business Communication: A Classroom Simulation* can be used with any textbook, or it can stand alone as the primary source.

ACKNOWLEDGMENTS

We wish to thank the following reviewers who gave us additional perspective on what we have tried to accomplish with this project:

- Roosevelt Butler, *Trenton State College*
- Randy E. Cone, *University of New Orleans*
- Karon Cunningham, *Southwest Missouri State University*
- Constance Dees, *Alabama Agricultural and Mechanical University*
- Debra J. Housel, *State University of New York at Brockport*

Your suggestions have been incorporated into this book.

Thanks also to Prentice Hall's Maureen P. Hull, editor for Business Education; Marianne J. Bernotsky, assistant to the editor; Robert Kern, Business Education marketing manager; and Marcia Krefetz, senior production editor, for their encouragement and direction on this project.

The best way to get the most out of this simulation and your business communication class is to get into the role that you play in your company. Take it seriously, and play according to the rules. You will find that you will begin to identify with your company early, taking pride in everything you and your team create. Enjoy the experience, and take advantage of this unique opportunity to sharpen your communication skills.

Jim Stull
John Baird

Business Communication:
A Classroom Simulation

Unit 1

COMMUNICATION IN ORGANIZATIONS:
GETTING BACK TO BASICS

Objectives

By successfully completing this unit, you will:

- understand the communication process;
- increase your ability to create messages that are clear, concise, complete, correct, coherent, concrete, and courteous (the Seven C's);
- know why you should select your words carefully;
- realize the importance of establishing and maintaining goodwill;
- learn correct formats for letters and memos; and
- be aware of opportunities to use electronic mail and other modern communication techniques.

Case Study

Aztech Assembly is a Mexico-based subsidiary of Excel Computers. Excel sends all of its computer components to Aztech, where the computers are assembled, packaged, and sent directly to retail outlets. Nearly all of the managers at Aztech were born and educated in the United States; all of the assembly personnel are from the local community.

Roberto Amezcua is an assembly-line supervisor. He is learning to speak English, but he has never been outside Mexico. He has attended a local technical college and is currently enrolled in Aztech's management training program. He is first in line for a promotion. Carol French is an electrical engineer from Excel who is visiting the assembly plant to explore the opportunity of upgrading the computer-assisted assembly process. She speaks just a few words of Spanish.

Because it is a hot afternoon, Carol decides to wear shorts and sandals to the plant. She takes a brief tour of the assembly line and talks with a few of the management staff. Then she walks over to Roberto's desk and says, "un momento, por favor," and motions for him to follow her. They enter a conference room.

1

__What are potential communication problems in this situation?__ Will Roberto and Carol be able to communicate about what Carol wants to do with the assembly line? Will any of the following be issues with either of them: language? role expectations? gender? how Carol communicated for Roberto to follow her? Carol's clothing? attitudes about each other's culture? any other issues? You might want to discuss this case with your classmates.

The Communication Process

Simply stated, **communication** is the process of sending and receiving messages. When you speak or write, you send messages; when you listen or read, you receive messages. You also send nonverbal messages through your body language and other behavior. Everything you do (including not doing anything) communicates something. One cannot *not* communicate.

You use words to represent ideas that exist in your mind. Assigning words to meaning is called **encoding.** The other person assigns meaning to the words you use. This is known as **decoding.** You want other people to get the same meaning out of your message that you have. When you believe this happens, you generally feel successful. Most communication is successful. It is important to keep in mind, however, that the message sent is *never* the message received. People's experiences differ. A word or phrase will mean something just a little different to you than it does to someone else. Of course, the greater these differences, the greater the chance for miscommunication.

The possibility of a communication breakdown exists in any situation. In business, people are "in the heat of battle," working toward company goals. Frequently, they are more concerned with getting the job done than with taking extra time to ensure that their messages will be "perfect." And who knows what makes a good message? Many people believe that as long as the message is communicated, it is successful. Many other people, however, realize that successful business communication involves more than merely getting the message across to other people.

Feedback will let you know if your message has been accurately understood. You receive feedback in different ways: from the person's behavior, from a verbal confirmation, by your asking questions, from other people, and more.

The Seven C's

You will increase the probability of your messages being understood if they are **clear, concise, concrete, correct, coherent, complete,** and **courteous.** These steps also increase the likelihood that your messages will help maintain harmonious relationships with others. While these concepts are usually discussed in terms of written messages, they are equally important in oral communication.

Clear

Your messages need to be clear if they are to be effective. Business people are usually very busy and want to know right away what you are trying to tell them. Many believe the saying, "time is money."

One way you can enhance the clarity of your messages is to use **simple words.**

WHY SAY?	WHEN YOU CAN SAY
contemplate	think, plan
equitable	fair
magnitude	size
is indicative of	shows, points out
facilitate	help

You can improve the clarity of your message by using more of the **active** (rather than passive) **voice.** A simple rule to follow when you are constructing sentences is to show your subject acting upon an object (subject-verb-object). For example:

WHY SAY?	WHEN YOU CAN SAY
The meeting was attended by the stockholders.	The stockholders attended the meeting.
The award was received by Jesse Sanchez.	Jesse Sanchez received the award.
The forms were sent this morning.	We sent the forms this morning.

You *might* want to use the **passive voice**, however, to de-emphasize the receiver's role in messages about negative situations. You will also be more **tactful** when you show this concern for your reader.

WHY SAY?	WHEN YOU CAN SAY
You did not send your payment for last month.	Last month's payment has still not been received.
	or
	Please send last month's payment.

Another way to clarify your messages is to use **short, simple sentences.** For example:

WHY SAY?	WHEN YOU CAN SAY
If you are able, please make every possible effort to have your response completed and sent to us no later than May 4.	Please respond by May 4.
Before you begin the checkout procedure, be sure to secure two copies of Form 198, which you'll find in the Purchasing Office; then fill in the form on the top half, get your supervisor's signature, and send the form to the Order Department.	Get two copies of Form 198. Complete the top half of the forms. Get your supervisor to sign them. Then send them to the Order Department.

Of course, you need to **strive for an appropriate balance of simple, compound, and complex sentences.** Also, be sure to write **short paragraphs.**

Concise

If you want your messages to be read by busy people, make them brief. Say what you need to say, and say no more (while maintaining goodwill, of course). Remove all words, phrases, and sentences that serve no purpose. One way to achieve this is to write your first draft, read it, restate your purpose in one sentence, and edit and rewrite your message to achieve that purpose. You can ensure conciseness in your writing by eliminating wordiness, overused expressions, and unnecessary redundancy.

Many unnecessary words in your sentences can take the punch out of your writing and result in messages that are difficult to understand. Strive to **eliminate wordiness.**

WHY SAY?	WHEN YOU CAN SAY
Should you have any questions in regard to the above matter, we will be glad to go over them at your convenience.	Please ask if you have any questions.
I would like to take the liberty of asking you that you grant me an interview.	May we set up an interview?
It is important that all managers follow the affirmative action guidelines that have been written in the procedures manual.	Managers must follow the affirmative action guidelines in the procedures manual.

You can also eliminate wordiness by **substituting one word for wordy, overused expressions.** For example:

WHY SAY?	WHEN YOU CAN SAY
in regard to	about
in view of the fact that	since
at all times	always
in the event that	if
at the present time	now
in order to	to
prior to the start of	before
due to the fact that	because
arrived at the conclusion	concluded
along the lines of	like
during the time that	while
are in a position to	can
in a very few examples	seldom

You can make your messages more concise by **eliminating meaningless expressions.** For example:

WHY SAY?	WHEN YOU CAN SAY
Per your request, here are . . .	Here are . . . you requested
It has come to my attention	*(eliminate completely)*
Please be advised that	*(eliminate completely)*
Permit me to say	*(eliminate completely)*
Enclosed herewith is; Enclosed please find	Here is
The author, the writer, the undersigned	I, me
Please don't hesitate to call.	Please call.

You can make your messages more concise by **avoiding unnecessary redundancy.** Is any meaning lost if the italicized words are removed from the following sentences?

Our meeting is scheduled for 7 p.m. *in the evening*.
Be sure to emphasize the *important* essentials.
We need to reach a *group* consensus.
Our forecast is based on *past* history.
Our product is *very* unique.
Each *and every* employee is eligible for a bonus.

Concrete

You have a choice in your writing to use concrete (specific) or abstract (vague) words. They both have a place in business writing. However, concrete terms are typically more accurate and, in some cases, more believable.

WHY SAY?	WHEN YOU CAN SAY
Please send your report within three weeks from today.	Please send your report by May 6.
Do you have any computer training?	Have you ever operated a Macintosh SE?
I have management experience.	I have managed a sales department with 25employees and an annual budget of over $2 million.
To whom it may concern:	Dear Ms. Fimbrez:

Correct

Correctness in business writing includes proper spelling, grammar, punctuation, and format. For spelling, punctuation, and grammar, you should keep a dictionary and a writer's guide at your desk.

The two most common types of business correspondence you will write are the letter and the memorandum or memo. Letters are typically written to people outside your company; memos are written to people inside. Following are examples of an acceptable format for each (Examples 1-1 and 1-2).

Computer World

2245 West Palm Drive, Silicon Valley, CA 95100

Marketing and Sales   (408)555-2245

Letterhead

_____

Date

June 5, 1991

**Inside
Address**

Mr. Gerald S. Jones
Vice President, Marketing
Interact Corporation
1654 Lancaster Boulevard
Boston, MA 02158

Salutation

Dear Mr. Jones:

Thank you for your letter of May 27, requesting
information on our latest line of computer products for
the SuperXL.

Body

Enclosed are our most recent brochures, price lists and a
flier on our current research.

When you order from us, you will receive a preferred
customer discount. We look forward to a long-lasting
relationship.

**Complimentary
Close**

Sincerely,

Signature

Marilyn S. Fong
Assistant Manager

**Author's/Typist's
Initials**

MSF/jbs

Enclosures

Example 1-1
Letter Format
(Block Style)

6

Computer World
Memo

June 30, 1991

Heading

To: Joseph Sanchez

From: Dan Lum

Subject: Personnel Meeting, July 6, 10:30 a.m., Conference Rm.

Body

Please plan to attend the Personnel Committee meeting next week.

We will discuss the criteria for merit increases and promotions. Please review your handbook and other materials before the meeting. Representatives from all employee units will be present.

Particularly, Joe, I would like you to be prepared to answer any questions on the procedures followed in determining who actually receives the increases and promotions.

I look forward to seeing you there.

Dan

Example 1-2
Memorandum Format

Coherent

Messages need to "hang together." Ideas need to flow from one to the next through smooth transitions. You can achieve this by outlining your message, writing simple sentences and focusing each paragraph on one idea. You can also improve the coherence of your message through **parallel structure, connecting words and phrases,** and **guide posts**.

When you want to express similar ideas with equal emphasis, use **parallel structure.** This applies to sentences or phrases. Use the same sentence structure and verb form for each separate idea.

WHY SAY?	WHEN YOU CAN SAY
It took some time to choose the team. Then we developed a plan and then finally the decision was made. All of this took six months.	Choosing the team, developing a plan, and making a decision took six months.
(from a résumé) • responsible for developing marketing plans for each year • in charge of supervision of sales team	• developed annual marketing plans • supervised 25 sales representatives

When you want to connect ideas, use **transition words and phrases.**

WHY SAY?	WHEN YOU CAN SAY
The book you ordered is out of print. We are returning your check. You may wish to contact a book search service for assistance.	The book you ordered is out of print. *Therefore*, we are returning your check. *However*, you may wish to contact a book search service for assistance.
Before we can reimburse you, you must complete a form. You must also attach all receipts to the form. Take the form to the Payroll Department. You might have to wait a couple of weeks for payment.	To get reimbursed, *first*, complete Form 3; *second*, attach all receipts to the form; *third*, submit your form to the Payroll Department; *then*, wait two weeks for payment.

You can also show how things are organized by using **guide posts**.

WHY SAY?	WHEN YOU CAN SAY
Our next Personnel Committee meeting is scheduled for Friday, May 31, at 4 p.m. in the Conference Room.	**WHAT:** Personnel Committee Meeting **WHEN:** Friday, May 31, 4 p.m. **WHERE:** Conference Room

Complete

Check to be sure that your message is complete. Have you included all the information you need to ensure that the other person can do a complete job or make a reasonable decision? Jot down all of the necessary details you wish to include in your message before you begin to write. Once you have written the message, go back and see if you have included all that is necessary. You may sometimes have to determine what to include and what to exclude to make your message effective.

WHY SAY?	WHEN YOU CAN SAY
Please plan to attend our meeting on Friday.	Please plan to attend our meeting on Friday *at 4 p.m.*
Please submit your cover letter and résumé to our Personnel Committee.	Please submit your cover letter, résumé, *and transcripts to Dr. Frieda Mendehlson, chair* of our Personnel Committee.

Courteous

Besides communicating your idea, your message also needs to enhance **goodwill**. Goodwill is the degree to which the person you are communicating with perceives you as likable and trustworthy. The relationship between you and your reader or listener is very important. You can build goodwill through a courteous tone in your messages.

Your messages should be **positive**. You should go through your messages and circle any words that might startle or alarm the other person; for example, no, never, not, cannot, don't, regret, inconvenience, problem, fail, avoid, difficult. Certain words and phrases can have a negative impact on readers. After a while, you'll be able to spot them and keep them out of your messages.

WHY SAY?	WHEN YOU CAN SAY
Your car will not be ready until Tuesday.	Your car will be ready on Tuesday.
We regret that since you closed your account, your name will be missing from our long list of satisfied customers. We sincerely hope that, despite the best efforts of our fine staff, there was no occasion on which we failed to serve you. Because you have not included your receipt, it is impossible for us to refund your money.	Thank you for letting us serve you. Please call on us again when you wish to open another account. Please submit your receipt so that you can receive your refund.
Employees with fewer than three years on the company payroll are ineligible for stock options	Employees with more than three years on the company payroll are eligible for stock options.

Your message should reflect the **you-attitude**, placing the reader as the focus of the message. If the message is negative, you may wish to avoid the you-attitude.

WHY SAY?	WHEN YOU CAN SAY
I want to send my congratulations.	Congratulations!
I want to express my appreciation.	Thank you.
We will ship your May 4 order today.	Your May 4 order is being shipped today.
We have enclosed a reply envelope.	Please use the enclosed envelope for your reply.
Since we have our obligations to meet, we must ask your immediate attention to your past-due account.	Please submit your payment to bring your account up-to-date.
You left the lathe running all night.	The lathe was on when I got here this morning. *(Avoid the you-attitude in negative messages).*

Be sure to **find out the appropriate title** for the other person. You may need to ask to see how people prefer to be addressed. Watch their reactions to your use of titles; you may not have to ask.

WHY SAY?	WHEN YOU CAN SAY
Dear Mrs. Gervais	Dear Ms. Gervais
Dear Ms. Gervais	Dear Dr. Gervais
Mr. Rodriquez	Mr. Rodriguez *(note spelling)*
Mr. Robert Rodriguez	Mr. Robert Rodriguez, Vice President of Marketing
Ms. Ramirez	Carlita *(when you know someone well)*

Your messages should **avoid gender bias.** For example:

WHY SAY?	WHEN YOU CAN SAY
gentlemen's agreement	informal agreement
manpower	human resources, workers
man hours	working hours, total hours
man-made	synthetic, manufactured

You are probably thinking that this is a great deal to remember each time you prepare a message. However, once you have developed sound business communication skills, you will automatically employ these concepts in your writing. Let's consider a situation to see how these concepts can be applied.

John Chambers is the vice president of manufacturing for Silicon Valley Computer Company (SVCC). SVCC is going to phase out its current Model 6789 and begin to manufacture Model 6799, a more powerful computer. They have always ordered the printed circuit boards for Model 6789 from Mountain View Supply Company. John's secretary, Maile, asks a management trainee, Mike, to write a letter for John to Carlita Ramirez, office manager at Mountain View Supply Company. John wants to tell her that SVCC will no longer order printed circuit boards for Model 6789 from her company. Example 1-3 is the first draft of his letter.

How effective is this letter? How would Carlita feel if she received a letter like this from a client and an organization that she had done business with for a number of years? The letter is not very effective and lacks many of the basics. Which of the Seven C's have not been applied here? Use this space to list as many examples as you can where the Seven C's could have been applied.

How could the Seven C's have been applied here?

Maile reads the first draft and tells Mike that she is having trouble determining the purpose of the message. She tells Mike to rewrite the message, making it more clear that SVCC will no longer order the parts for Model 6789. She also tells him to cut out all of the unnecessary words, and to watch spelling, punctuation, and grammar. Mike is a little frustrated because he believes he has done a good job. He has tried to be businesslike in his phrases and has tried to be like the manager he wants to be some day. Mike sits down and rewrites the letter and comes up with a second draft (Example 1-4).

11

Silicon Valley Computer Company
One Washington Square
Silicon Valley, CA 95192

June 21, 1993

Carlita Romeerres, Manager
Mountain View Supply Company
2 North Avenue
Mountain View, California

Dear Miss Romeeres,

In the business of high technology change is inevitable and I'm sure just as you are that your company goes thru just as many changes as our company goes thru. As you are well aware, when nobody bys your products any more you have to make changes or else you go out of business. This is a major concern with us. We want to stay in business because we have been so successful. We need to move into others areas so we can keep up with the competition. When our sales were down with our Model 6789 we knew we had to do something about it, so we speont alot of time researching what to do to be sure we would stay in business. Now we have decided to manufacture another model which will require a whole bunch of new parts.

We have enjoyed doing business with you during the passed few years and hope you'll be successfull in the future with other purchasers of your parts. If I can clarify this message or if something doesn't make sense, please don't hesitate to call me.

Sincerely,

John Chambers, V.P.
Manufacturing

Example 1-3
Letter Without the Seven C's

Silicon Valley Computer Company
One Washington Square
Silicon Valley, CA 95192

June 21, 1993

Carlita Romeeres, Manager
Mountain View Supply Company
2 North Avenue
Mountain View, California

Dear Ms. Romeeres,

Silicon Valley Computer Company regrets to inform you that we will no longer order
parts for our Model 6789. We hope this won't be an inconvenience to you.

Do not hesitate to call if you have any questions.

Sincerely,

John Chambers

John Chambers, V.P.
Manufacturing

Example 1-4
Concise, Clear Letter Without Courtesy and Correctness

13

While Mike's second draft is concise and the purpose is clear, it could use more diplomacy and a few corrections. It could start off by indicating that the relationship with Carlita and Mountain View Supply has been a good one through the years. Mike might move more gradually into the news that SVCC will no longer need the parts because the computer is being discontinued.

The letter is still negative and does nothing to leave Carlita with a positive feeling. The letter does not make use of the you-attitude. Mike might have indicated possible interest in other parts for additional products being developed. He could show Carlita that John is aware of the negative consequences of this situation and that things may work out in the future. The letter ends in a very pat way with little effort to establish the goodwill necessary. Maile tells Mike that Carlita is John's long-time business associate, and that John would never treat her in such a cold, formal manner. She also tells Mike to spell her name correctly. Mike takes out his dictionary and college business communication book and "fine tunes" the letter.

What changes would you make to Mike's second draft?

Let's see how the letter might look after one more draft (Example 1-5).

14

Silicon Valley Computer Company
One Washington Square
Silicon Valley, CA 95192

June 21, 1993

Ms. Carlita Ramirez, Office Manager
Mountain View Supply Company
Two North Avenue
Mountain View, CA 94043

Dear Carlita:

Mountain View Supply Company and Silicon Valley Computer Company have enjoyed a successful business relationship for the past several years. You and I have survived many changes in the computer industry, and you have always been there to serve SVCC.

SVCC Model 6799 will be available in computer stores on August 1. It is more powerful than Model 6789, and a whole new line of compatible software is being developed by Programs International. The future of this innovation looks bright, and you deserve to share in its growth.

We have already modified our production process for Model 6799. The mother boards for the new computer differ from those previously ordered from you, so we have signed a six-month contract with the manufacturer of the new boards. Because our relationship is so important, we wish to continue to order other parts from you and will consider ordering the new mother boards if you carry them by the end of this year.

Thanks for your continued service and dependability. I look forward to the opportunity to continue working with you during these exciting times.

Sincerely,

John Chambers, V.P.
Manufacturing

Example 1-5
Is This Any Better?

15

Now, compare all three letters. Study them. What can you say about each? The first letter contains problems related to all Seven C's. As we've moved through these examples, we've tried to remove many of their faults. While Example 1-3 should be regarded by most readers as the best of the three letters, much of what you see here has to be processed through your own filter. You have your own preferences about how you communicate. You may find that some of these techniques don't fit your style, particularly regarding courtesy. You may want to be wordier or more direct. That's your decision. Consider which of the Seven C's allow for variation and which do not. Then, develop the best communication skills you can to fit your individual needs.

Electronic Communication

One final point about sending business messages is important here. So many messages are sent electronically. Many of the situations you will encounter in this simulation might be handled more quickly on the telephone. Other messages would be written at the computer keyboard and sent through electronic mail. Teleconferencing could take the place of a face-to-face business proposal meeting. Your business communication course and this simulation are designed to get you to write more and to be aware of using the language more effectively. If you find that the logistics of completing the assignment go against your common sense—that is, if you would telephone someone rather than write a letter or memo—complete the assignment for the purpose of developing your writing skills.

Below are several exercises to help you sharpen your communication skills. Work through as many as necessary. Be sure to ask your instructor for guidance.

Exercises

Clarity

Rewrite the following passages so that they are **clear**.

1. The parameters of our endeavor substantiate the need for more communication.

2. My perception of the problem indicates a need for a viable plan that facilitates the realization of bottom-line results.

3. A young specimen of the masculine gender and his female counterpart ambulated up a rather colossal precipice. They were in hopes of attaining a specified amount of fluid which is desirable for consumption by human beings. To continue, the aforementioned male apparently lost his equilibrium and as a result descended to the terrestrial surface at a rapid and uncontrollable rate. His cranium suffered extensive damage. The feminine member of the escapade followed suit and plunged down the same incline.

4. As you can probably determine from my enclosed resume I have gained some experience in the field through one or maybe two of my previous jobs, depending upon whether you regard volunteer experience as really experience just because it wasn't a paid job. Anyway, the experience I had in some of the bookkeeping areas that you described in your job announcement seem to be quite similar to what I did during both my real job and my volunteer job. The paid one was more posting and entering data on a sort-of computer type machine, but the other one was more interesting because I actually got to work in accounts payable for a week.

And, of course, I have taken a semester of accounting in college where I was able to work many problems that have prepared me well for a job in the accounting area.

5. One of the things we have to do in this company is to determine how best we can make the best use of all employees so that they believe that we care about them, particularly our new immigrants from other lands where business practices differ so much from the way we practice them in the United States with our western way of life.

Conciseness

Rewrite the following wordy passages. Be **concise**, and maintain tact and diplomacy through use of the "you attitude" and positive wording.

1. Let me remind all of you employees of the necessity and importance of your being sure that you begin your work day on time at eight o'clock each and every morning and that you are sure not to leave any time before five o'clock in the afternoon.

2. I just want to congratulate you on your truly superb and fantastic performance during this past fiscal year; your work was exemplary and will serve as a model for all of your fellow colleagues to try to follow as they carry out their responsibilities in the organization.

3. When giving feedback to one of your employees, as a manager you should always remember to tell employees when they have done well in a manner so that others are aware of the good performance; on the other hand, if you must tell the employee that the performance level needs improvement or modification in some way, you should always remember that the appropriate way that will make the employee feel better about the feedback and more than likely will respond more favorably is if you take precautions to ensure that the feedback is always carried out in the confines of a secluded, private environment.

4. It should be observed that not very many, in fact only 15, cases of absenteeism took place in the second month of this year, which was February; this was the very month, in fact, when the new system was begun.

5. We found after careful investigation and research that several different organizations and companies were satisfactory and offered programs which were designed to improve the ability of our engineers in the vital and important areas of report writing.

6. We have found that many customers of this firm have been quite concerned and upset by our new policy on deliveries. This new delivery policy requires a minimum order from each and every customer; these orders are to have a minimum dollar value of $50.

7. The University Placement Office has sent me at periodic intervals a form inquiring as to my current employment status. As you may recall from our discussion last spring I was most desirous of making a favorable change in vocational locale. After following up several recommendations made by your office (Goodwin, etc.) I was unable to negotiate an immediate change, and upon receiving suave assurances of rapid promotion from my superiors promptly regressed into the torpid complacency which characterized my thinking upon graduation. However, my present intention to move is more than a harbinger of that most fragrant of seasons but rather stems from a feeling of disillusionment and inadequacy with my vocational environment.

May I once again prevail upon you to assist me in this undertaking by informing me at your convenience of any job opportunity for which you think I would be well suited. As indicated in my last reply to your office, I no longer look to accounting as my forte but instead am seeking a selling situation which is both challenging and remunerative.

Thank you for your patience and understanding in this matter. You may reach me at 555-1234 during the day or at 555-4321 in the evening.

Concreteness

Reword the following sentences so that meaning is **less abstract and more specific**. Pay attention to the italicized words.

1. Please try to have your response mailed back to me by *three weeks from today*.

2. We need to complete an order to get *some* new computers for the office.

3. I was active in *sports* during college.

4. My favorite subjects in school were in the *social sciences*.

5. The job will require that you perform *accounting functions*.

6. I want you to complete *some* major projects today.

7. Please have enough materials for *some* guests who will be visiting *this week*.

8. Would you please go into the mail room, see what's wrong with *that machine* in there, and order *a part* for it.

9. Be sure to seat Mrs. Cummings on the *right* side of the room.

10. Yes, I have *international business* experience.

Correctness

The following exercises will help you develop messages that have correct grammar and punctuation.

Punctuation Punctuate the following sentences. When you are finished, check the key that follows. If you are having difficulty with a particular type of punctuation, seek help from a punctuation guide or your instructor.

1. When you send your purchase order use the following address 246 Technology Drive Silicon Valley CA 95192

2. Its obvious Ms Fleishman that the secretaries desks must be ordered within a weeks time

3. It is of course important for Mr Gonzales Ms Tran and Ms OBrien to attend Ms Luchettis planning session

4. The teams decision therefore must be turned in to the personnel officers office by 1130 this morning

5. The assembly line supervisor shouted stop the machines however nobody heard him and Johns hand was injured

6. If you think you are entitled to be reimbursed for your expenses take your receipts to payroll not accounts payable

7. Carlo Cetti our new sales manager has been scheduled to start on July 1 but he will travel with one of our sales representatives for two days

8. In their book Prentice Hall Handbook for Writers Leggett Mead and Kramer include a few examples of business correspondence it is however geared more toward the general writer not the business writer

9. Walking into the lobby this morning I noticed the date on the calendar was December 31 somebody needs to change it

10. Our delivery route includes London England Madrid Spain Rome Italy and Paris France

11. Our new warehouse supervisor survived his probationary period sometimes however I wish we had let him go

12. Why do you indicate the amount of money by the word alot not a real word when you mean a lot asked the manager she explained that the word allot meaning to apportion has two ls

13. Your boss told me that the commissions from everyone elses contracts should be yours because you did all the work

14. All of our retail outlets particularly those in Los Angeles and St Louis should consider staying open on New Years Day

15. During the first quarter of the year profits were high the boards decision to give early bonuses therefore was an appropriate one.

Underline the words that would be correct in the following sentences:

16. (Their, There, They're) sure that (you're, your) decision was the correct one.

17. (Its, It's) become far too common that the washroom key has been removed from (its, it's) proper place.

18. Surely (your, you're) promotion will mean that (your, you're) planning to transfer to (their, there, they're) new office before (its, it's) grand opening.

19. (Whose, Who's) scheduled to interview the applicants and read (their, there, they're) résumés?

20. (Its, It's) not on (your, you're) appointment schedule; (whose, who's) responsibility is it?

Key to punctuation exercise :

1. When you send your purchase order, use the following address: 246 Technology Drive, Silicon Valley, CA 95192.

2. It's obvious, Ms. Fleishman, that the secretaries' desks must be ordered within a week's time.

3. It is, of course, important for Mr. Gonzales, Ms. Tran, and Ms. O'Brien to attend Ms. Luchetti's planning session.

4. The team's decision, therefore, must be turned in to the personnel officer's office by 11:30 this morning.

5. The assembly line supervisor shouted, "Stop the machines!"; however, nobody heard him, and John's hand was injured.

6. If you think you are entitled to be reimbursed for your expenses, take your receipts to payroll, not accounts payable.

7. Carlo Cetti, our new sales manager, has been scheduled to start on July 1, but he will travel with one of our sales representatives for two days.

8. In their book, *Prentice Hall Handbook for Writers*, Leggett, Mead, and Kramer include a few examples of business correspondence; it is, however, geared more toward the general writer, not the business writer.

9. Walking into the lobby this morning, I noticed the date on the calendar was December 31; somebody needs to change it.

10. Our delivery route includes London, England; Madrid, Spain; Rome, Italy; and Paris, France.

11. Our new warehouse supervisor survived his probationary period; sometimes, however, I wish we had let him go.

12. "Why do you indicate the amount of money by the word 'alot'—not a real word—when you mean 'a lot'?" asked the manager. She explained that the word "allot" (meaning to apportion) has two l's.

13. Your boss told me that the commissions from everyone else's contracts should be yours because you did all the work.

14. All of our retail outlets, particularly those in Los Angeles and St. Louis, should consider staying open on New Year's Day.

15. During the first quarter of the year profits were high; the board's decision to give early bonuses, therefore, was an appropriate one.

16. (Their, There, They're) sure that (you're, your) decision was the correct one.

17. (Its, It's) become far too common that the washroom key has been removed from (its, it's) proper place.

18. Surely (your, you're) promotion will mean that (your, you're) planning to transfer to (their, there, they're) new office before (its, it's) grand opening.

19. (Whose, Who's) scheduled to interview the applicants and read (their, there, they're) résumés?

20. (Its, It's) not on (your, you're) appointment schedule; (whose, who's) responsibility is it?

Sentence Structure Too many simple sentences can make messages sound choppy. Change the following simple sentences to compound or complex sentences. Be sure to punctuate them properly.

1. Here is our check for $250. It represents an overpayment on your account.

2. Your charge limit is $2,500. You can request that we extend it after six months.

3. Customers will respond to professional salespeople. You should attend our seminar on effective selling.

4. Larry Garcia is an expert on international marketing. He has lived and worked in three different countries during the past 10 years.

5. You must work as an accountant for at least five years. It is the only way you can become an accounting manager in this company.

6. He joined our company this year. He hopes to be promoted to supervisor by January.

7. She went to the finance seminar last week. She didn't have enough time to learn everything.

8. She chose the Macintosh. The IBM had more software available. Everyone else in her office uses a Macintosh.

9. You will do well in this company if you work hard. You might get promoted.

10. There are many good reasons to hire Sally. It may be difficult to do.

Correct the following sentences:

11. The plant will be open every weekday, only the security office will be open on weekends.

12. Zack didn't show up for work today. Because he stayed up late watching television.

13. You keep track of new accounts, I'll keep track of current ones.

14. Mr. Lopes is in a meeting Ms. Kumara is in Memphis Ms. Akbayan is in charge of the office.

15. Tom Schwartz is attending a trade conference. In a city where he has never been.

21

Key to sentence structure exercises:

Some of these sentences can be written in more than one way.

1. Here is our check for $250, which represents an overpayment on your account. *or* Here is our check for $250; it represents an overpayment on your account. *or* Because you overpaid your account, here is our check for $250.

2. Your charge limit is $2,500; however, you can request that we extend it after six months. *or* Although your charge limit is $2,500, you can request that we extend it in six months.

3. Customers will respond to professional salespeople; therefore, you should attend our seminar on effective selling. *or* Because customers respond to professional salespeople, you should attend our seminar on effective selling.

4. Larry Garcia is an expert on international marketing; he has lived and worked in three different countries during the past 10 years. *or* Because he has lived and worked in three different countries during the past 10 years, Larry Garcia is an expert on international marketing.

5. You must work as an accountant for at least five years; it is the only way you can become an accounting manager in this company. *or* If you want to become an accounting manager in this company, you must work as an accountant for at least five years.

6. He joined our company this year; he hopes to be promoted to supervisor by January. *or* Although he joined our company just this year, he hopes to be promoted to supervisor by January.

7. She went to the finance seminar last week, but she didn't have enough time to learn everything. *or* Although she went to the finance seminar last week, she didn't have enough time to learn everything.

8. She chose the Macintosh, even though the IBM had more software available, because everyone else in her office uses a Macintosh. *or* Although the IBM has more available software, she chose the Macintosh because everyone else in her office uses one.

9. You will do well in this company if you work hard; you might even get promoted. *or* If you work hard, you will do well in this company; you might even get promoted.

10. There are many good reasons to hire Sally; however, it may be difficult to do. *or* While there might be many good reasons to hire Sally, it may be difficult to do.

11. The plant will be open every weekday; only the security office will be open on weekends.

12. Zack didn't show up for work today because he stayed up late watching television.

13. You keep track of new accounts; I'll keep track of current ones.

14. Mr. Lopes is in a meeting; Ms. Kumara is in Memphis; so Ms. Akbayan is in charge of the office.

15. Tom Schwartz is attending a trade conference in a city where he has never been.

Parallel Structure   Rephrase the following sentences to achieve parallel structure.

1. To improve your business communication, you should learn about grammar, letter styles, and how to address the reader properly.

2. When you prepare your résumé for an employer, you should be sure to select a good quality paper, decide what you want to include, organize the material for maximum effect, and typing it so that it is as neat as possible.

3. Not only males but also those who are female can become chief executive officers in business.

4. Business people know that problems can be solved more quickly by analyzing them than ignoring them.

5. At the company picnic, most people spent their time swimming, playing softball, dancing, and ate the lunches they brought with them.

Key to parallel structure exercise:

1. To improve your business communication, you should learn about grammar, letter styles, and addressing the reader properly.

2. When you prepare your résumé for an employer, you should be sure to select a good quality paper, decide what you want to include, organize the material for maximum effect, and type it so that it is as neat as possible.

3. Not only males but also females can become chief executive officers in business. *or* Both males and females can become chief executive officers in business.

4. Business people know that problems can be solved more quickly by analyzing them than by ignoring them.

5. At the company picnic, most people spent their time swimming, playing softball, dancing, and eating the lunches they brought with them.

Modification   Rewrite the following sentences to correct the modification and to eliminate ambiguities.

1. After she prepared the letter, the manager invited her secretary to accompany her to lunch.

2. The automobile manufacturer recalled the models from the customers that had defective parts.

3. While cleaning off my desk last night, the cover letters were somehow misplaced.

4. Offices are sometimes assigned to new employees that are shabby, dim, and cold.

5. Before showing you how to operate this copy machine, your manuscript needs some corrections.

Key to modification exercise:

1. After the secretary prepared the letter, his manager invited him to lunch.

2. The automobile manufacturer recalled the defective models from its customers.

3. While cleaning off my desk last night, I misplaced the cover letters.

4. Shabby, dim, and cold offices are sometimes assigned to new employees

5. Before I show you how to operate this copy machine, your manuscript needs some corrections.

Subject-Verb Agreement   Underline the correct verb in each of the following sentences.

1. There (is, are) usually 14 people present at the meeting.

2. Parts for the typewriter (comes, come) from the stockroom.

3. Each of these parts (is, are) available in the supply room.

4. Alex and Marnie (spend, spends) far too much time making decisions.

5. Either of the supervisors or the typist (is, are) eligible for the award.

6. My manager and mentor (follow, follows) my progress closely.

7. Carla or Michael (is, are) taking care of appointments today.

8. The committee (is, are) making a decision about your promotion today.

9. One of the group's decisions (is, are) to replace the insurance plan.

10. My main interest in this decision (is, are) sound ethics.

Key to subject-verb agreement exercise:

1. There (is, <u>are)</u> usually 14 people present at the meeting.

2. Parts for the typewriter (comes, <u>come</u>) from the stockroom.

3. Each of these parts (<u>is,</u> are) available in the supply room.

4. Alex and Marnie (<u>spend,</u> spends) far too much time making decisions.

5. Either of the supervisors or the typist (<u>is,</u> are) eligible for the award.

6. My manager and mentor (follow, <u>follows</u>) my progress closely.

7. Carla or Michael (<u>is,</u> are) taking care of appointments today.

8. The committee (<u>is</u>, are) making a decision about your promotion today.

9. One of the group's decisions (<u>is</u>, are) to replace the insurance plan.

10. My main interest in this decision (<u>is</u>, are) sound ethics.

Pronoun Agreement Rewrite any of the following sentences that show incorrect or ambiguous pronoun agreement.

1. Sally took her secretary back to the bookstore to get her credit card.

2. Neither the stockholders' report nor the latest *Wall Street Journal* will include that information in their contents.

3. The committee made its decision today.

4. Every manager is responsible for their decisions.

5. We must plan to renovate both the offices and the factory building because its foundations are weak.

Key to pronoun agreement exercise:

1. Sally took her secretary back to the bookstore to get Sally's (*or* the secretary's) credit card.

2. Neither the stockholders' report nor the latest *Wall Street Journal* will include that information in its contents.

3. The committee made its decision today. *(Correct, if the decision is collective)*

4. Every manager is responsible for his or her decisions. *or* Managers are responsible for their decisions.

5. We must plan to renovate both the offices and the factory building because their foundations are weak.

Coherence

Rewrite the following passages so that they are more easily understood. Fill in the blanks with **transitions, enumerations, guide posts,** or other connecting words.

1. For many students, majoring in business is synonymous with getting rich. _____, what so many don't realize is that getting rich takes a great deal of hard work and vision. _____, getting rich is not a good reason to go into business. _____, people ought to put more thought into why they are in school.

2. I can think of a number of good reasons why you should type the report. _____, it will look better. _____, it demonstrates a professional attitude. _____, it will be easier to revise in the future. _____, your handwriting is hard to read.

25

3. When you move into your new office, you need to arrange the furniture so that you get the maximum use out of the space you have available, putting pictures on the wall will help add a personal touch, and ask the boss to give you a new carpet and computer.

Courtesy

Here is an actual letter written by a representative of a well-known food manufacturer. Can you rewrite it so that it is **more positive?**

> Thank you for informing us of your experience with a Mrs. Smiths® Cherry Pie. We do not like to have dissatisfied customers, but we do appreciate your taking the time to contact us.
>
> We are concerned when a customer finds a pie in an unsatisfactory condition. This improperly filled pie probably occurred near the beginning or end of processing this particular variety and should have been removed from the pie line. Your letter has been referred to our plant manager for his review and corrective action. Our pie fillings have not been reduced in quantity, and we will continue to market high quality products. We are sorry for this unfortunate incident.
>
> To thank you for your interest in our Company, enclosed is a product coupon. We hope that you will continue to enjoy our products in the future.

The following message was used by a department store to retrieve credit card customers who had cancelled their accounts. Can you make it sound **more positive and diplomatic?**

> We were sorry to learn that your name will be missing from our list of Bergmann's credit card customers.
>
> Now you will be unable to have the spending power that you once had. This might prove to be an inconvenience to you.
>
> We hope we have not failed to serve you. If you change your mind, do not hesitate to call us so that we may reopen your closed account.

"You-Attitude" Rewrite the following sentences, using the **"you-attitude."** Try to involve your reader.

1. We have completed the work on your car.

2. Our warranty on the work is good for 90 days.

3. I wish you would send me your résumé.

4. We've mailed a check.

5. Our savings accounts pay 6 percent interest.

6. To help me process this order, I must ask for another copy of the purchase requisition.

26

7. We are please to announce our new flight schedule from Silicon Valley, which is every hour on the hour.

8. We offer the printer ribbons in five colors.

9. I have seven years' experience as a sales representative.

10. We have put all of our demo models on sale to make room in our showroom for next year's models.

11. Our research and development team has worked for three years to develop our newest bran cereal, which we feel will give people the fiber they need.

12. We believe we have the best fabrics on the market.

13. We also sell accessories that can be matched with any suit.

14. We are eager to have you try our new lipstick that we just added to our line.

15. We have been selling real estate in Silicon Valley for 50 years.

16. We have flexible scheduling of ours at our company, so that we can offer our employees the shifts of their choice.

17. We would like to put your name on our customer list to get advance notice of our sales.

18. We have a 125-piece tool set that comes with a free tool box.

19. We follow a policy that each customer has 90 days to act on a warranty.

20. We like to encourage our employees to participate in our decisions.

Positive Writing Rewrite the following sentences so that they are **positive** and demonstrate **goodwill**.

1. It is impossible to repair this television today.

2. We apologize for inconveniencing you during our remodeling.

3. The problem with your account is that you failed to make your payment last month.

4. You filled out your order form wrong. We can't send you the parts you need until you tell us which parts are broken.

5. Your saw doesn't work because you spilled coffee into the motor while it was running.

6. There can be no exceptions to this policy.

7. I've heard a lot of silly ideas since I've been working here, but this is the silliest I've ever heard.

8. You really fouled things up with the last computer run.

9. Smoking is not permitted anywhere except outside the building.

10. You've had my order for four weeks. When are you going to deliver my couch?

11. You failed to tell us what size pizza you want.

12. We cannot deliver your lumber until next Thursday.

13. I am afraid you miscalculated your payment on your May bill.

14. We are not able to process your order accurately when your forms are filled out incorrectly.

15. Because you failed to send back your toaster within the six-month warranty period, we cannot honor your request for a total refund.

16. We regret to inform you that we must deny your request for credit with Bergmann's.

17. You are wrong in your claim, for the warranty clearly states that you must return your vegetable slicer within 30 days if you are not satisfied.

18. Pretty Kitty doesn't get stinky and clumpy like other cat litter.

19. Please don't hesitate to call if you have any problems.

20. I know I haven't had much experience in accounting and that I won't graduate until May, but I would like to be considered for the job.

Rules for Good Writing

Each is the following rules for good writing has at least one mistake in it that demonstrates a violation of that rule. Rewrite each sentence. Have fun doing this; it's meant to be humorous.

1. Subjects and verbs always has to agree.

2. Do not use a foreign term when there is an adequate English *quid pro quo*.

3. It behooves the writer to avoid archaic expressions.

4. Do not use hyperbole; only one writer in a million can use it effectively.

5. Avoid clichés like the plague.

6. Mixed metaphors are a pain in the neck and should be thrown out the window.

7. Placing a comma between subjects and predicates, is not correct.

8. Parenthetical words however must be enclosed by commas.

9. Consult a dictionary frequently to avoid mispelling.

10. Don't be redundant or say what you have already said before.

11. Remember to never split an infinitive.

12. Never use a preposition to end a sentence with.

13. The passive voice should be avoided.

14. Use the apostrophe in it's proper place and omit it when its not needed.

15. Don't use no double negatives.

16. Proofread carefully to see if you have any words out.

17. Hopefully, you will use words correctly irregardless of how others use them.

18. Never use a long word when a diminutive one will do.

19. Avoid colloquial stuff.

20. No sentence fragments.

21. One criteria for good writing is whether you recognize such words as "data" and "media" as plurals.

22. Eschew obfuscation.

23. Remember to finish what you

A Goodwill Letter

Your company is interested in sponsoring interns from the local university to learn more about your organization. These interns could perform many marketing, manufacturing, management, and personnel jobs. The students would be business majors and would provide you with good labor at a very good price. You are interested in the possibility of hiring some of these interns if they work out well. Write a letter to the dean of the school of business at your local university asking him or her to explore the internship possibility with you. Remember, this is a letter of goodwill. Be sure to follow the principles discussed in this unit. **Write your letter in the space provided on the next page.**   After you have done this, **edit** your first draft, indicating the specific areas for improvement. Finally, **rewrite** your message based on your editing. Is your rewrite an improvement? How is it better? Can improvements still be made?

First Draft

Second Draft

30

Proofreader's Marks

gr	=	grammar
sp	=	spelling
//	=	parallel construction needed
cliché	=	avoid using clichés
⁀	=	transpose (was it = it was)
red	=	redundant
♪	=	flag word
ww	=	wrong word
wc	=	questionable word choice
tense	=	wrong verb tense
div	=	word divided wrong
margins	=	margins should be wider/narrower
ss	=	single-space these lines
ds	=	double-space these lines
4sp	=	type your name four lines below complimentary close
←	=	move this to the left, right, up, down (direction of arrow)
⟋	=	delete this
center	=	center this (vertically or horizontally)
^	=	insert (job done = job well done)
^?	=	something is missing here
line up	=	line up these items (vertically or horizontally)
agr	=	subject/verb/object agreement
you att	=	needs more "you-attitude"
prep	=	avoid ending sentence with preposition
¶	=	start a new paragraph
lc	=	use lowercase (small) letters
caps	=	use uppercase (capital) letters
frag	=	sentence fragment (incomplete sentence)
^#	=	insert a space (typedreport = typed report)
⊂	=	close up (every body = everybody)
awk	=	awkwardly constructed phrase/sentence/paragraph
neg	=	sounds negative; make it sound positive
ret add	=	include your return address
date	=	include the date
sig	=	be sure to sign this
spl inf	=	avoid splitting verb infinitives (to report, to manage, etc.)
action	=	use an action verb; avoid forms of "to be"
ESL	=	problems with English as a second language
___	=	underline or italicize (foreign words, book titles, etc.)

> *. . . about the simulation. . .* In Unit 2 you will actually form companies and learn about corporate culture. Each person in your company will serve in a position as president or vice president. You will write an introduction letter to each of your counterparts in the other companies. You will want to incorporate all of the concepts discussed in Unit 1 on how to write effective business messages. Your company team will develop a brochure or corporate culture statement about your company. You will present your company and meet your counterparts at the Silicon Valley Fair.

Unit 2

INTRODUCTION TO THE SIMULATION:
DEVELOPING CORPORATE CULTURE

Objectives

By successfully completing this unit, you will:

- learn the background for the simulation;
- join a company for which you will work;
- determine your position and responsibilities within that company;
- understand the concept of corporate culture;
- create and communicate a corporate culture; and
- apply the principles of writing goodwill messages.

Background to Simulation

You are about to become involved in a very exciting way to learn about business communications: the simulation approach. This simulation has been tested since 1987 with hundreds of business students. Students find that the approach pulls them into learning in a way that promotes interest and motivation to learning.

Simulations are a popular and widely used method of teaching and training people in the development of various skills. Discoveries about aircraft in flight have been made in wind tunnels. Astronauts train for space flight through simulations. Airplane pilots and automobile drivers learn on simulators. Law students experience trial conditions through moot courts. First-aid personnel practice cardiopulmonary resuscitation on inflatable dummies. Security, safety, and medical personnel train to deal with various hazards and obstacles through fire drills, lifeboat drills, air raid drills, disaster training, and other forms of simulation.

Simulations have also been used widely in management training. Machine and interpersonal simulations have given trainees ideas about what to expect and how to react to probable leadership situations.

What is a simulation? A simulation is an exercise in which participants are assigned roles to play in order to practice what might naturally occur in a given setting. If participants are unfamiliar with their roles, the simulation permits them to learn the constraints and responsibilities of those roles.

Get ready for a fun learning experience! It will be difficult not to get involved in the simulation you are about to experience. The structure of this process will help you develop skill in business communication while providing you with a strong sense of the realities of the business world.

Company Scenarios

You will join one of six companies that are connected as part of the simulation network. The following companies are used in the simulation:

- a manufacturing company
- an assembly company
- a supply company
- a software development company
- a retail store chain
- a public relations company

These companies all interact in the competitive business environment. The **manufacturing** company is the largest of the companies and manufactures a very successful personal computer. The **assembly** company is an offshore assembler of computers. This company is part of the parent manufacturing company and receives parts from the supply company. The **supply** company manufactures many of the parts used in the personal computers and supplies parts to the assembly company and the software development company. The **software development** organization develops programs for personal computers in coordination with the manufacturer, the assembler, the supplier and the retail chain. The **retail store chain** in one of the largest chains in the country, selling computers, accessories, software, and other state-of-the-art equipment. The **public relations** company is a U.S.-based consulting firm specializing in advertising, public relations and marketing research for high-tech organizations. The following scenarios are designed to give additional background information about the companies.

The Manufacturing Company

Company Background The firm was founded by William and David Masters about 20 years ago. Both men were graduates of a very prestigious engineering program and were interested in the development of a personal computer that would revolutionize our society. Within a few years, they had developed a product and founded a company with a net worth that would grow to $5 billion within 10 years. The Masters brothers still hold a very strong grip on the company, and their quest for innovations in the computer business has helped keep the company on top. The company is international in scope, with offices and manufacturing facilities all over the world. With increased manufacturing costs in the United States, the company has placed more emphasis on an offshore manufacturing strategy. The firm owns a Mexico-based assembly plant.

Products, Services, and Developments The company has been most successful in the education market with the recently introduced XL503 personal computer. Recently, the business strategy has involved the penetration of large business accounts interested in networking personal computers. A portable computer is about to be introduced. Software development continues to be an important aspect of the business. The firm is considering the purchase of a very successful software development organization. The development of a computer notebook concept is one of the product innovations of high priority.

Financials This is a $5 billion company with profits of $250 million in the past year. The company is cash rich, with over $1 billion in the bank. Some industry analysts believe that the company is ripe for being bought by one of the computer giants. The company has experienced rapid growth (15 percent to 25 percent) over the last five years. There is some speculation that with the market a bit flat, its growth will not continue to be so dramatic.

According to the Analysts The analysts have always been high on this company. However, the firm seems so interested in the business end of the market that there has been little new product development in the education market. Employees are beginning to complain about the lack of vision and direction for the company. Over the last year, three senior-level managers have left the organization. The firm has grown so much over the last few years that some analysts say that it is not responding to innovations and change as quickly as it used to. Products are taking longer and longer to get to market.

Notes:

Manufacturing Company Positions

President   Calls executive staff meetings • handles personnel matters • distributes all mail to employees • coordinates all company projects • communicates with all the other company presidents

Vice President of Marketing   Coordinates all marketing functions within organization • manages product marketing strategy in company • supervises any survey or data analysis projects • communicates with all the other marketing vice presidents and the vice president of manufacturing accounts for the public relations company

Vice President of Overseas Operations   Coordinates all overseas operations • plans overseas operations strategy • deals with personnel issues related to overseas operations • communicates with the vice president of relations with manufacturers for the assembly company; vice president of overseas operations for the supplier company; vice president of relations with assemblers for the software development company; vice president of relations with assemblers for the retail store chain; and the vice president of assembler accounts for the public relations company

Vice President of Software Development   Coordinates all software development activity within the company • responsible for software development strategy for company • coordinates all research and development activities • communicates with all of the other software development vice presidents; vice president of relations with software development for the retail store chain; vice president of software accounts for the public relations company

Vice President of Purchasing   Coordinates all purchasing activity within the organization• establishes all purchasing rules and regulations for the company • negotiates all major purchasing contracts between companies • communicates with vice president of purchasing for the assembly company; vice president of relations with manufacturers for the supplier company; vice president of relations with suppliers for the software development company; vice president of relations with suppliers for the retail store chain; vice president of supplier accounts for the public relations company

Vice President of Retail Operations Coordinates all retail operations activities within the organization• meets regularly with retail operations personnel from other companies• plans retail operations strategy for the company • communicates with all the other retail operations vice presidents; vice president of relations with retailers for the software development company; vice president of relations with manufacturers for the retail store chain; vice president of retail accounts for the public relations company

Notes:

The Assembly Company

Company Background The assembly company is a Mexico-based assembler of computers. The firm receives components from suppliers and assembles computers for manufacturers, including the parent company, the manufacturer of the XL503. The company was established by the parent manufacturing company to deal with the rising costs of manufacturing in this country. The company is run by executives from the United States with a great deal of control from the parent company. Turnover of executives is high because such a job is a stepping stone for high-level positions back in the United States. The parent company has invested a great deal in the development of innovative manufacturing techniques designed to increase the quality of the products as well as the efficiency of the manufacturing process. There are 200 employees, most of whom are locals from the Mexican communities surrounding the plant.

Products, Services, and Developments The company is not involved in a great deal of research and development, except in the area of improvement of manufacturing techniques. The plant is new, with all the current manufacturing innovations. The plant has instituted some very effective quality improvement programs that have served as models for the industry. Employee participation programs have been most effective in improving productivity and employee morale.

Financials The company has helped the parent organization with its profit margins. Company growth has been over 40 percent over the last three years, and is expected to continue as the parent company decides to manufacture more computers in offshore facilities. The parent company will continue to invest more money into this facility in order to keep the manufacturing at the highest quality.

According to the Analysts The analysts have not had much to say about this company, except in reference to the increased profitability of the parent company. One analyst expressed concern about the small number of locals in management. There seems to be little effort to develop the local talent to move into supervisory and management positions within the company.

Notes:

37

President Calls executive staff meetings • handles personnel matters • distributes all mail to employees • coordinates all company projects • communicates with all the other company presidents

Vice President of Marketing Coordinates all marketing functions within organization • manages product marketing strategy in company • supervises any survey or data analysis projects • communicates with all the other marketing vice presidents and the vice president of assembler accounts for the public relations company

Vice President of Relations with Manufacturers Coordinates all manufacturing activities • plans and organizes manufacturing strategy for organization • communicates with all vice presidents of overseas operations ; vice president of relations with assemblers for the software development company; vice president of relations with manufacturers for the retail store chain; vice president of manufacturing accounts for the public relations company

Vice President of Software Development Coordinates all software development activity within the company • responsible for software development strategy for company • coordinates all research and development activities • communicates with all of the other sdoftware development vice presidents; vice president of relations with manufacturers for the software development company; vice president of relations with software developers for the retail store chain; vice president of software accounts for the public relations company

Vice President of Purchasing Coordinates all purchasing activity within the organization • establishes all purchasing rules and regulations for the company • negotiates all major purchasing contracts between companies • communicates with all of the other purchasing vice presidents; vice president of relations with manufacturers for the supplier company; vice president of relations with suppliers for the software development company; vice president of relations with suppliers for the retail store chain; vice president of supplier accounts for the public relations company

Vice President of Retail Operations Coordinates all retail operations activities within the organization • meets regularly with retail operations personnel from other companies • plans retail operations strategy for the company • communicates with all the other retail operations vice presidents; vice president of relations with retailers for the software development company; vice president of relations with assemblers for the retail store chain; vice president of retail accounts for the public relations company

Notes:

The Supply Company

Company Background The supply company is only seven years old. It furnishes computer manufacturers with components to go into their computers, assemblers with components to be used in the assembly of the computers, software developers with printed circuit boards to go along with the software, and retailers with replacements parts for computers. The CEO is a technological genius who has helped the company with many innovations in the printed circuit area. The firm employs 150 people and prides itself on having a very "family-oriented" atmosphere, with many semi-skilled workers from Mexico, Guatemala, Nicaragua, El Salvador, Vietnam, China, and the Philippines. A great deal of growth is expected in the future, with plans to double in size over the next few years.

Products, Services, and Developments The company has developed a patent on a printed circuit design that has become one of the standards for the market. This design has given the company a strong technological edge in the marketplace. Other standard computer parts are manufactured, but most of the money comes from the sale of printed circuit boards. The company supplies some of the major computer firms with their component parts. Research and development are top priorities, and the CEO continues to sink all profits into this area. The company is considering the possibility of manufacturing its own computers, although the market is rather flat and highly competitive. This debate over getting into the computer manufacturing business is one that has caused a great deal of conflict in the organization.

Financials The company is close to going public; most expect that this will happen within the next few years. The firm has experienced 30 percemt to 40 percent growth rates over the past couple of years and realized profits of approximately $650,000 this past year. The expectation is that profits will double over the next three years.

According to the Analysts The analysts are very high on this company and are confident that the firm will indeed go public within the next few years. There is some concern that the computer market is going flat and that profits will not be as great next year. However, analysts are continually impressed with the way that the company is managed and the amount of resources targeted to research and development. There is no agreement by analysts on the issue regarding the interest of the company to manufacture its own personal computers.

Notes:

President   Calls executive staff meetings • handles personnel matters • distributes all mail to employees • coordinates all company projects • communicates with all the other company presidents

Vice President of Marketing   Coordinates all marketing functions within organization • manages product marketing strategy in company • supervises any survey or data analysis projects • communicates with all the other marketing vice presidents and the vice president of supplier accounts for the public relations company

Vice President of Overseas Operations   Coordinates all overseas operations • plans overseas operations strategy • deals with personnel issues related to overseas operations • communicates with the vice president of relations with manufacturers for the assembly company; vice president of overseas operations for the manufacturing company; vice president of relations with assemblers for the software development company; vice president of relations with assemblers for the retail store chain; vice president of assembler accounts for the public relations company

Vice President of Software Development   Coordinates all software development activity within the company • responsible for software development strategy for company • coordinates all research and development activities • communicates with all of the other software development vice presidents; vice president of relations with suppliers for the software development company; vice president of relations with software development for the retail store chain; vice president of software accounts for the public relations company

Vice President of Relations with Manufacturers   Coordinates all purchasing activity within the organization • establishes all purchasing rules and regulations for the company • negotiates all major purchasing contracts between companies • communicates with vice presidents of purchasing; vice president of relations with manufacturers for the software development company; vice president of relations with manufacturers for the retail store chain; vice president of manufacturing accounts for the public relations company

Vice President of Retail Operations   Coordinates all retail operations activities within the organization • meets regularly with retail operations personnel from other companies • plans retail operations strategy for the company • communicates with all the other retail operations vice presidents; vice president of relations with retailers for the software development company; vice president of relations with suppliers for the retail store chain; vice president of retail accounts for the public relations company

Notes:

The Software Development Company

Company Background   This company is one of the largest in the country specializing, in the development of software for personal and business computers. The firm was founded by Charles Whitworth, a genius in developing software applications. He developed a highly successful word processing package that put the company on the map. The firm now enjoys a 40 percent share of the software market. The company works closely with computer manufacturers, suppliers, retail stores, and assemblers in order to develop the best quality software applications. An international sales force has helped penetrate foreign markets. Profits from foreign sales are expected to double over the next two years.

Products, Services and Developments   The company develops software for business, educational, and home applications, and it has developed some specific applications for the XL503 personal computer. If this personal computer continues to sell as well as expected, the new software applications will help the company's profits this year. The company is in the process of developing a new software package called *Integrate,* a unique software package that integrates special graphics with spreadsheet and word processing advances. A great deal of money is spent on research and development. A strong customer feedback program helps in the product development phases. The company manages an extensive international hotline for customers with questions regarding their software.

Financials   This $5 billion company has enjoyed high levels of profit over the last five years. The stock remains strong; however, the uncertainty of the personal computer market has caused some fear among investors.

According to the Analysts   Analysts have been high on this company for a long time. It has begun to mature without showing a dip in profits. Most analysts agree that the company has introduced excellent products and has some interesting new ones in the development stage. The competition has a difficult time delivering the kind of products and service that this company has made its hallmark. Analysts question the company's ability to maintain its high levels of growth and profits because of flat personal computer sales over the past few months.

Notes:

Software Development Company Positions

President   Calls executive staff meetings • handles personnel matters • distributes all mail to employees • coordinates all company projects • communicates with all the other company presidents

Vice President of Marketing   Coordinates all marketing functions within organization • manages product marketing strategy in company • supervises any survey or data analysis projects • communicates with all the other marketing vice presidents and the vice president of software accounts for the public relations company

Vice President of Relations with Assemblers   Coordinates all overseas operations • plans overseas operations strategy • deals with personnel issues related to overseas operations • communicates with the vice president of relations with manufacturers for the assembly company; vice presidents of overseas operations for the manufacturing and supplier companies; vice president of relations with assemblers for the retail store chain; vice president of assembler accounts for the public relations company

Vice President of Relations with Manufacturers   Coordinates all software development activity within the company • responsible for software development strategy for company • coordinates all research and development activities • communicates with the software development vice presidents for the manufacturing and assembly companies; vice president of relations with manufacturers for the supply company and the retail store chain; and the vice president of manufacturing accounts for the public relations company

Vice President of Relations with Suppliers   Coordinates all purchasing activity within the organization • establishes all purchasing rules and regulations for the company • negotiates all major purchasing contracts between companies • communicates with vice presidents of purchasing; vice president of software development for the supply company; vice president of relations with suppliers for the retail store chain; vice president of supplier accounts for the public relations company

Vice President of Relations with Retailers   Coordinates all retail operations activities within the organization • meets regularly with retail operations personnel from other companies • plans retail operations strategy for the company • communicates with all the other retail operations vice presidents; vice president of relations with software development for the retail store chain; vice president of retail accounts for the public relations company

Notes:

The Retail Store Chain

Company Background This company has been a very successful U.S.-based retail chain, selling computers, accessories, software, and other state-of-the-art equipment. Each store in the chain has a parts and service center as well as education and training for customers. Close relationships are fostered with all the major computer manufacturers. A hot item at the present time is the XL503 personal computer. The company was established 10 years ago by a group of computer experts who all decided to leave their companies and start a computer retail business. The chain started with one store but now has close to 150 stores nationally. The company is planning to add two new stores this year. The company was established on the premise that service makes the difference. This philosophy has been important in helping the company remain profitable over the last five years.

Products, Services, and Developments The company continues to add new services to its stores. The parts and services center has increased profitability. Also, the addition of the education and training service is beginning to see payoffs for the company. This service is being expanded on a pilot basis to businesses interested in additional training and education for their employees.

Financials The company has seen a leveling off of the huge growth in profitability that occurred over the last five years. The is a $5 billion company whose plans are to approach the $10 billion range over the next few years. The key to this strategy is the opening of new stores. First-quarter earnings indicate that the company may not be profitable this year. The slow computer business is having a direct impact on retail sales. The company hopes that the new XL503 will help profitability.

According to the Analysts The analysts are not as high on this company as they once were. There is some concern that the company has grown too quickly and has tried to add too many stores at a time when the market is just not there. The stock has taken a continual decline over the last few months; some speculate that the company will not be profitable this year. Some analysts are concerned that the once fabled service has been replaced with concern for increased profits and growth. Also, the firm has put all its eggs in the XL503 basket; few other personal computer products are selling well. Analysts are concerned that the company needs to push other products and diversify its sales strategy.

Notes:

Retail Store Chain Company Positions

President   Calls executive staff meetings • handles personnel matters • distributes all mail to employees • coordinates all company projects • communicates with all the other company presidents

Vice President of Marketing   Coordinates all marketing functions within organization • manages product marketing strategy in company • supervises any survey or data analysis projects • communicates with all the other marketing vice presidents and the vice president of retail accounts for the public relations company

Vice President of Relations with Assemblers   Coordinates all overseas operations • plans overseas operations strategy • deals with personnel issues related to overseas operations • communicates with the vice president of relations with manufacturers for the assembly company; vice presidents of overseas operations for the manufacturing and supplier companies; vice president of relations with assemblers for the software development company; vice president of assembler accounts for the public relations company

Vice President of Relations with Software Developers   Coordinates all software development activity within the company • responsible for software development strategy for company • coordinates all research and development activities • communicates with all of the other software development vice presidents; vice president of relations with retailers for the software development company; vice president of software accounts for the public relations company

Vice President of Relations with Suppliers   Coordinates all purchasing activity within the organization • establishes all purchasing rules and regulations for the company • negotiates all major purchasing contracts between companies • communicates with vice presidents of purchasing; vice president of relations with manufacturers for the supplier company; vice president of relations with suppliers for the software company; vice president of supplier accounts for the public relations company

Vice President of Relations with Manufacturers   Coordinates all retail operations activities within the organization • meets regularly with retail operations personnel from other companies • plans retail operations strategy for the company • communicates with all the other retail operations vice presidents; vice president of relations with manufacturers for the software development company; vice president of manufacturing accounts for the public relations company

Notes:

The Public Relations Company

Company Background This company is a U.S.-based firm specializing in advertising, public relations, and marketing research. Founded in New York, the firm quickly established a reputation for being one of the premier advertising organizations in the country. The company has created advertising campaigns for some of the most successful high technology companies in the world. The client list includes all the other companies in this simulation. The company has offices in London and Paris. Alana Shubert inherited the company from her father, and as CEO she has doubled the size of the company and helped begin to establish an international presence. Her leadership has been innovative and "bottom-line"-oriented.

Products, Services, and Developments The company offers basic consulting services in the areas of advertising, public relations, and marketing. The firm specializes in data-gathering methods designed to give high quality, reliable information about markets and market trends to customers. The company has been attempting to diversify its services and has begun to move into the management consultation services. The company has just finished a very successful quality improvement project for a major high technology organization. This project involved training managers in quality improvement management skills.

Financials   Profits have continued to climb over the last few years as the company approaches the $1 billion category by the end of the year. The company is in a position to be taken over by one of the larger public relations firms, and there has been a great deal of talk about this issue.

According to the Analysts   The analysts are a bit concerned about the profits for this year. The first quarter showed a 10 percent drop in profits for the first time. The company claims that a few major clients dropped their accounts because of the sluggish computer economy. The analysts are encouraging the company to begin to diversify its account base as soon as possible. There is speculation that Alana Shubert is going to retire at the end of the year, and there has been no indication of who her successor will be. The firm's stock has lost significant value over the last couple of months.

Notes:

President   Calls executive staff meetings • handles personnel matters • distributes all mail to employees • coordinates all company projects • communicates with all the other company Presidents

Vice President of Manufacturing Accounts Coordinates all marketing functions within organization• manages product marketing strategy in company • supervises any survey or data analysis projects • communicates with all vice presidents of relations with manufacturers; vice president of marketing for the manufacturing company

Vice President of Assembler Accounts   Coordinates all overseas operations • plans overseas operations strategy • deals with personnel issues related to overseas operations • communicates with the vice president of marketing for the assembly company; vice presidents of overseas operations for the manufacturing and supplier companies; vice president of relations with assemblers for the software development company; vice president of relations with assemblers for the retail store chain

Vice President of Software Accounts Coordinates all software development activity within the company • responsible for software development strategy for company • coordinates all research and development activities • communicates with all of the other software development vice presidents; vice president of marketing for the software development company; vice president of relations with software development for the retail store chain

Vice President of Supplier Accounts Coordinates all purchasing activity within the organization •   establishes all purchasing rules and regulations for the company • negotiates all major purchasing contracts between companies • communicates with vice presidents of purchasing; vice president of marketing for the supply company; vice president of relations with suppliers for the software company; vice president of relations with suppliers for the retail store chain

Vice President of Retail Accounts Coordinates all retail operations activities within the organization • meets regularly with retail operations personnel from other companies • plans retail operations strategy for the company • communicates with all the other retail operations vice presidents; vice president of relations with retailers for the software development company; vice president of marketing for the retail store chain

Notes:

The Development of Corporate Culture

During this unit, you will prepare two assignments, both designed to help you write more effective goodwill communications. The first assignment is an introduction to corporate culture, which involves a one-page public statement about the corporation's culture. Each company will present a 10-minute presentation introducing the company.

The second assignment is a letter of introduction written by each of you to your counterparts in the other companies. Both assignments will help you improve your skill in writing communications to develop goodwill. A detailed description of each of these assignments follows.

The Nature of Corporate Culture

Imagine yourself walking into an organization where there are no separate offices. There are only partitions, creating an open-office environment. There are plants in the building and very attractive wall decorations. Everyone is dressed casually, and it is difficult to tell the employees from the managers.

This example illustrates a few aspects of corporate culture. Over the last decade corporate culture has become a very popular concept. There are many organizational development experts who have written extensively about it. There are major differences between the corporate cultures of an Apple Computer and a General Motors.

The Elements of Corporate Culture.

In their book *Corporate Cultures*, Terrence Deal and Allan Kennedy discuss four internal elements of culture: values, heroes, rites and rituals, and the cultural network.

Values   Values are the foundation of any corporate culture. Values express the philosophy of the organization and provide structure and direction for the way in which work is accomplished. For example, at Hewlett-Packard, the "H-P Way" expresses the importance that the company places on teamwork and individual opportunity in the organization. Hewlett-Packard prides itself on high employee morale, opportunities for advancement, and an "open-door" policy.

Heroes   Heroes are very important to the understanding of corporate culture. Heroes are usually visionaries who have had a major impact on the culture of the organization. Apple's founder Steve Jobs was a visionary whose impact on Apple is still apparent. His philosophy of creative work combined with play helped Apple attract valuable talent to the organization. Even with his exit from Apple, this aspect of the culture can still be seen. These heroes have great insight about the vision of products, but they also have definite notions about the way work should be done.

Rites and Rituals   Rites and rituals provide interesting information about the culture of an organization. Tandem Computers instituted a traditional Friday afternoon "beer blast" to help celebrate the major accomplishments of the week or month. These gatherings have become part of the ritual at Tandem. They also provide a way for management to give personal recognition to employees. Rituals provide clues as to the degree of formality or informality in an organization. The meetings conducted in organizations vary in many ways: frequency, time of day, setting (room and table arrangements), make-up of the group, and the nature of the interaction. Rites and rituals help employees socialize to an organization and communicate a great deal about what the organization considers important.

Cultural Network The cultural network refers to the way in which information is communicated in the organization. Some organizations place great emphasis on company newsletters and publications. Others make extensive use of one-on-one meetings, while some companies place high value on the use of team meetings. Also, the cultural network is important in determining who is part of the communication network. We all know that the formal communication network and the organizational chart do not tell the entire picture. How are decisions communicated informally? Why is it that some of the most influential people in the organization are not necessarily on the organizational chart? They have informal power and are major players in the cultural communication network.

All of these aspects, values, heroes, rites and rituals, and the cultural network, make up what is known as corporate culture. Corporate culture embodies the basic assumptions that a particular company has discovered or developed in order to deal with the social adaptation of its members. Corporate culture helps us understand what an organization values as important, as well as the way in which the work is accomplished.

Homework Problems

Corporate Culture Statement

Culture is the way of life of a group of people; corporate culture is the way of life within a corporation, including its language, philosophies and values, rites and rituals, folklore, heroes, rules, politics, technology, communication practices, interpersonal relationships, and more.

Understanding the culture of the corporation you work for helps you identify better with the organization, perform your task to meet the organization's mission, feel better about the organization, and behave according to the rules of the organization.

"Excellent" organizations have identifiable cultures with clear guidelines about the organization's mission. Logos and slogans are selected carefully and displayed so that clients, customers, and employees are constantly reminded about the organization's concern for product quality, people, or service as reflected in the organization's superordinate goal statement.

After you have been introduced to corporate cultures, you will be given a brief description of your organization, the other organizations in the simulation, and the roles to be played by each member of your organization.

Expand upon the information given to you and develop a one-page public statement about your corporation's culture. This document will be distributed to each member of the class. It may include your company name and logo, names and titles of your officers, and information about your mission, philosophy, management style, products, etc. You should create company stationery that you will use for all written messages in the simulation.

On the due date you will make a **10-minute presentation**, introducing your company, its members, and your culture to the other companies. In preparing for this assignment, your company may want to use the questions in the following Corporate Culture Guide.

Corporate Culture Guide By answering the following questions about your company, you will gain greater insight into its culture. This is your chance to be creative and to create an image for your company that you will be able to maintain or modify throughout the simulation. Many of these questions require much time and thought before you will reach an answer that satisfies each member of your team. Be sure to address other questions that arise as a result of this exercise.

1. What is the name of your organization? The name might reflect your company's mission, technology, products, founder(s), or anything that you want it to communicate to the public, your employees, stockholders, etc.

2. Have you designed a logo? What does it mean? Does it reflect anything special about your company?

3. What is the mission of your company? What does your company do?

4. Does your company have a statement or slogan that communicates an important company values to your employees, customers, stockholders, etc.?

5. Does your company have any rites or rituals (special events, ceremonies, practices that are never changed, etc.)?

6. What are the characteristics of the typical hero or role model in the company? What does it take to become a hero? Who has survived and is revered by others?

7. What would be the characteristics of a "loser" in your company? What types of people don't tend to survive here?

8. What is the communication network? Is this the formal network? the informal network? What is your communication policy?

9. How might insiders describe your company? How might outsiders describe your company? How might these descriptions differ? Why?

10. What information do you intend to include in your corporate culture statement?

11. Do your employees need to know any special jargon? company rules? company politics? Do you have orientation and training programs?

12. How would you classify your organization?

___ You gotta be tough to survive in this company.

___ We work hard, but we play hard, too.

___ We don't know if we'll be here tomorrow.

___ We'll be here forever; so will our paperwork.

___ *(other)*_____

13. What other things do you believe important to identify or express about your company?

Notes:

Sample Corporate Culture Statement   Following is a sample corporate culture statement. You may wish to include more information, but this gives an idea how brief it can be and the types of information you can put in it once you have answered some of the questions in the Corporate Culture Guide. After you read the following statement, refer to the previous questions to see which ones are answered in the statement.

ADVANCED TECHNOLOGY COMPONENTS
ONE WASHINGTON SQUARE
SAN JOSE, CA 95192
(408) 988-7800

"It is what's inside that counts!" This popular principle applies to people and especially to computers and software. The best computer and software are only as good as the components inside. Advanced Technology has always been on the forefront of high technology and has been serving Silicon Valley with the finest quality state-of-the-art components for over 10 years. For over a decade, our relentless goal has been to provide only the most technologically advanced components at the most competitive prices.

ATEC is the first company in the valley to help customers remain competitive through just-in-time delivery service, helping firms keep storage costs down. Never again would your schedule be set back due to late shipment of supplies. ATEC is there when you need us! We deliver on time to your assembly plants, with your exact specifications. With our constant JIT deliveries, you increase profits by keeping storage costs down. Always engaged in technological breakthroughs, we are the sole distributor of the most advanced VLSI (very large scale integrated) components. We constantly update our inventory and select as well as manufacture the latest advancements in chip and component science.

Each ATEC employee is meticulously trained to serve your needs and is seriously interested in doing business with you. Each one is trained to help you with your selections for your manufacturing, assembly, and software needs. Each ATEC associate puts *your needs first* in priority because *your needs are our deadlines.* We also believe in helping our manufacturing research and development by working with you and providing you with the most advanced materials to experiment with. Our prices are competitive so that you profit by keeping your supply costs down.

We merge your needs with the most advanced technology. Let ATEC be your stepping stone to the future.

WE GO BEYOND STATE OF THE ART

Example 2-1
Sample Corporate Culture Statement

Introduction Letter

Once your company is formed and your position is determined, write a letter to your counterparts in the other companies. Introduce yourself and your company to those with whom you will communicate during this semester.

Another purpose of this letter is to create goodwill. Be sure to get the names and addresses of your counterparts, and spell their names correctly. Your tone should be positive and personal. You should also be sure to use the "you-attitude" in this letter.

The following suggestions may help you structure a good letter:

1. Begin on a positive note. Introduce yourself and your company in the first paragraph; indicate the purpose of your letter. Resist the temptation to start with "Allow me to introduce myself; my name is Jane Doe; I am President of. . . ." Be creative and professional; find a unique way to begin your letter.

2. Give some background about the company. Refer to some of the goals and philosophies established by your team.

3. Describe your position, responsibilities, and goals and expectations about your working relationships with your counterparts, perhaps including a brief idea of the "ideal working relationship."

4. End on a positive note, indicating that you are looking forward to meeting on *(specify date)*, at *(specify time)* at *(specify location)*.

5. Since you must write letters to several counterparts, your letter may be identical, but you must change the names and company address. Use an appropriate business letter format. Be sure to submit a copy of one of the letters to your instructor.

Notes:

CREATIVE IDEAS

One Washington Square
San Jose, CA 95192
(408) 988-7800

October 15, 1993

Mr. Harvey Tokunaga
Vice President of Marketing
Excel-Tech, Inc.
One Washington Square
San Jose, CA 95192

Dear Mr. Tokunaga:

Silicon Valley is presently experiencing a competitive market in the computer technology industry. Creative Ideas may be able to help your company meet these competitive challenges and help contribute to your company's continued success.

Creative Ideas is a consulting firm specializing in public relations, advertising, and marketing research. We have a talented and knowledgeable staff that may accommodate the needs of your company in one or all of the following areas:

- Develop creative advertising campaigns;

- Establish channels of communication between your company and the public;

- Achieve desired results of publicizing the release of a new product; and

- Research and develop new ideas.

The philosophy of Creative Ideas is to inform the public of your product by way of mass media communication. The combination of your products and our strategies may result in the name of Excel-Tech becoming an everyday word in business.

I have reserved October 15, 1993, at 9:30 a.m. to meet with you for brunch at San Jose State University, Business Classroom 312. Please contact my office to confirm this date and time.

Cordially,

Pat Gross
Vice President of Manufacturing Accounts

Example 2-2
Sample Introduction Letter

53

Unit 3

EMPLOYMENT COMMUNICATION:
CREATING MESSAGES THAT GET THE JOB

Objectives

By successfully completing this unit, you will:

- learn more about the job-search process;
- write a position vacancy announcement;
- learn to use various formats in putting together a résumé;
- write an employment cover letter;
- interview for a job;
- write follow-up letters after the interview; and
- interview others for jobs.

Case Study

Sandy Jenkins has just finished her MBA and is looking for a job in the sales and marketing area. She visits the Career Planning and Placement Office at her university and comes across a position vacancy announcement for a job at Software Innovation, an international software programming company. The position looks as if it would be a good fit in that the company is looking for someone to develop and implement a marketing program in the company. The job will involve marketing research, with opportunity for international travel. Sandy is excited about the job and is ready to put her résumé together. She has a good employment background but very little experience in the high-tech area. She is not sure what format to use for her résumé.

Conducting the Job Search

Sandy will need to gather some specific information in order to make her résumé effective. Getting a job involves finding out as much about the job and the company as possible. The more information you have, the better your résumé will be in targeting the company and the position. Successful job candidates uniformly echo the value of gathering information before deciding how to put together the résumé.

Find out about the job. You need to begin by finding out about the position and what it involves. Sometimes a call to the company helps you clarify the position. You might ask some of your professors what the job might involve. Talk to people you know who might be in positions like this. Go to the library and consult the *Dictionary of Occupational Titles* for a general description of just about any position you might want to know about.

Find out about the company. For each company with which you plan to interview, you should find out its position in the market, what it does, its financial position, and its organizational structure. The library staff can help you gather information from current periodicals, stockholders' reports, government documents, and other sources. You may wish to contact the company directly and ask it for the current stockholders' report showing financial data regarding the company's performance for the year. Any current information on company philosophy or current product developments will give you an edge.

Find out about yourself. Knowing your own strengths and weaknesses can be a help in the employment process. If you know what you want and are able to articulate your objective, you will be more successful in matching the job to your needs. Your university placement office may administer a series of diagnostic tests to help you assess your own strengths and the jobs appropriate to these strengths. Employers are highly attracted to candidates who seem to have a clear direction and focus.

Writing the Résumé

Once you have conducted an appropriate job search, write your résumé. Writing your résumé requires presenting yourself on paper in the best possible way. For many jobs, the résumé is where the employer gets the first impression of you. It is important that the résumé be:

- easy to read,
- attractive to the eye,
- organized in a way to emphasize your strengths, and
- clear, in terms of your objective.

In preparing your resume, it is important that you do the following:

EMPLOYMENT RÉSUMÉS

- Select an appropriate heading
- Determine your objective
- Decide on an appropriate format for organizing your   experience
- Detail your education and extracurricular activities
- Pay attention to layout and style

Select an appropriate heading. You should place your name, address, and telephone number at the top of your paper. There are many different ways to present this information, and your choice will be a matter of personal style. A few examples follow:

James Moore
321 State Street
West Lafayette, Indiana 47906
(317) 555-4347

or

James Moore
321 State Street, West Lafayette, Indiana 47906 (317) 555-4347

or

James Moore

Temporary Address	Permanent Address
321 State Street	5456 Northridge Ave.
West Lafayette, IN 47906	Macon, GA 31204
(317) 555-4347	(912) 555-8028

Examples of Résumé Headings

Determine your objective.   The objective is one of the most important aspects of your résumé. Employers like to see applicants who know what they want to do. If you are certain about your objective, state it specifically (first example). If you are not sure about your objective, you may choose more general terms to state it (second example).

OBJECTIVE: Sales representative with opportunities for advancement to marketing manager.   *(more concrete terms)*

OBJECTIVE: Entry-level marketing trainee position with opportunities for advancement.   *(more general terms)*

Examples of Résumé Objectives

One argument against being too specific about the objective in a résumé is that you may limit your chance of getting a job when an opening exists for a job for which you are qualified but you have excluded yourself through your specificity.   On the other hand, if you are too general in your objective, employers may not feel that you have given your career much thought. The decision must be made on the basis of the job itself. You should indicate short- and long-term objectives, using such words as "growth," "opportunities for advancement," "forward-looking company," and other dynamic phrases.

Decide on an appropriate format for organizing your employment experience.   When you describe your job-related experience, you will need to ask yourself these questions:

• Do I want to list my specific jobs?

• Do I want to include a capsule statement that highlights my employment history?

• Do I want to list the jobs in the order I have held them? (a **chronological** résumé)

• Do I want to list the jobs that are related to my objective separately from other jobs? (a **functional** résumé)

• Do I want to highlight what I have achieved in the past that will apply to my current objective? (an **action** résumé)

The chronological résumé is one of the most frequently used formats. You generally list your work experience in reverse chronological order, presenting the most recent job first. An example of this format is presented below:

EXPERIENCE: Food server, The Whaler Restaurant, West Lafayette Indiana (1987-present)

• Developed strong communication and public relations skills
• Coordinated scheduling and inventory
• Created employee work-efficiency program

Assembler, Solar Cell, Inc., Indianapolis, Indiana (1986-87)

• Constructed solar panels
• Managed inventory
• Developed ability to work well with others
• Earned award for outstanding performance

Cook, McJack's Restaurant, Evansville, Indiana (1985-86)

• Prepared food for customers
• Managed food inventory
• Maintained good employee relations
• Earned seven Employee-of-the-Month awards

Retail Clerk, Mason's Department Store, Evansville, Indiana (1983-84)

• Managed inventory
• Created merchandise displays
• Developed strong customer relations skills
• Sold housewares

Example of Chronological Organization

The functional résumé groups similar jobs together. By placing related experiences together, you may create a clearer picture of your qualifications. Consider this as a possible functional approach for a sales representative position:

EXPERIENCE: <u>Food server, The Whaler Restaurant</u>, West Lafayette,
(SALES)   Indiana (1987-present)

- Developed strong communications and public relations skills
- Coordinated scheduling and inventory
- Created employee work efficiency program

<u>Retail Clerk, Mason's Department Store</u>, Evansville, Indiana
(1983-84)

- Managed inventory
- Created merchandise displays
- Developed strong customer relations skills
- Sold housewares

(OTHER)   <u>Assembler, Solar Cell, Inc.</u>, Indianapolis, Indiana (1986-87)

- Constructed solar panels
- Managed inventory
- Developed ability to work well with others
- Earned award for outstanding performance

<u>Cook, McJack's Restaurant,</u> Evansville, Indiana (1985-86)

- Prepared food for customers
- Maintained food inventory
- Maintained good employee relations
- Earned seven Employee-of-the-Month Awards

Example of Functional Organization

The action résumé presents a capsule of your work experience and uses action statements to show what you have achieved in all those jobs combined. This format is particularly appropriate when you want to de-emphasize the jobs while emphasizing the general skills and achievements you gained from those jobs. This format is useful when you lack specific experience for the job in question, as you can see from the example on the next page.

EXPERIENCE:
- Developed strong communication skills
- Trained personnel
- Established inventory re-order procedure
- Reported month-end and year-end sales figures
- Maintained positive customer relations
- Gained expertise in product and service knowledge

Food server, The Whaler Restaurant, West Lafayette, Indiana (1987-present)

Assembler, Solar Cell, Inc., Indianapolis, Indiana (1986-87)

Cook, McJack's Restaurant, Evansville, Indiana (1985-86)

Retail Clerk, Mason's Department Store, Evansville, Indiana (1983-84)

Example of Action Organization

Action words give life to your résumé as you highlight your accomplishments. You should carefully choose different action words that capture the essence of your accomplishments. Here is a list of some action words:

accomplished	doubled	interviewed	provided
achieved	earned	invented	raised profits
administered	engineered	justified	reconciled
analyzed	enlarged	keynoted	recorded
arranged	established	led	reduced
assisted	equipped	licensed	reduced costs
built	evaluated	maintained	reorganized
clarified	executed	managed	reported
completed	expanded	mastered	researched
conceived	experienced	mediated	served
conducted	financed	motivated	simplified
constructed	formed	negotiated	sold
consulted	formulated	nominated	solved
controlled	generated	operated	sparked
converted	gradruated	ordered	succeeded
coordinated	guided	organized	supervised
correlated	halved	originated	tailored
created	headed	overcame	trained
delegated	implemented	participated	transformed
demonstrated	improved	performed	unified
designed	increased	pioneered	united
detailed	initiated	planned	verified
developed	innovated	prepared	won
devised	inspired	produced	wrought
directed	integrated	promoted	wrote

When you use these action verbs, you should strive for specificity; that is, include numbers and details when possible.

- Trained and supervised 25 employees at retail sporting goods store.
- Raised $5,300 for local Red Cross chapter during earthquake relief drive.
- Developed three-day leadership training program for Beta Alpha Psi officers.
- Served as chairman of budget planning committee for Associated Students.

Detail your education and extracurricular activities. Under **education**, list only what is relevant to the job you are seeking: the schools from which you earned or plan to earn degrees, the degrees that you have received or anticipate receiving very shortly, your major, your minor (if applicable), and the year you earned or anticipate earning your degree (optional). This is likely all the information that you will need. However, some people like to include honors or their grade point average in this section if it is particularly high. Some like to exclude the date. Here are two examples:

EDUCATION: B.S.   Wayne State University (1993)
                              Major: Marketing
                              Minor: Communication Studies

EDUCATION: B.S.   Wayne State University
                              Major: Marketing
                              Minor: Communications Studies
                              G.P.A.: 3.98 *(Magna Cum Laude)*

Examples of Education Section

Your **extracurricular activities** and interests are usually presented as the final section of the résumé. This section would not be included if you wanted to use more space for job experience. Extracurricular activities can show the employer that you are well-rounded and how you choose to spend your spare time. These aspects are often used by employers during the interview to stimulate conversation. Whether you include this section is your choice.

Pay attention to layout and style. Once you have organized your résumé, you are now ready to think about its layout and style. It is important that you select a good quality paper. White, beige, gray, and pale blue are particularly good colors to choose. You can use a variety of type styles to highlight sections of your résumé, but the general rule is not to use too many.

In summary, a good résumé should include the following features:

- one or two pages in length;
- balanced set-up;
- good use of white space; and
- scannable format (reader should be able to scan résumé in six to eight seconds).

Refer to the case presented on page 53. The following résumé attempts to incorporate many of the principles discussed so far. What do you think of the résumé? What suggestions would you make for improvement?

61

SANDY JENKINS
1203 Nevada Avenue San Jose, CA 95125 (408) 555-4949

OBJECTIVE: Position in sales or marketing using proven leadership, analytical, communication, and intercultural skills.

EDUCATION: M.B.A. San Jose State University, May 1990
B.S. San Jose State University, December 1987
Major: International Business
Minors: Economics and Italian Language

EXPERIENCE: **Contract Administrator**
Department of the Air Force (1990-present)

Administrative Assistant
Ferrari Export Company (1984-1987)

Travel Consultant
Trans World Airlines (1981-1984)

Marketing and Sales

Researched and evaluated market opportunities
- Interviewed businesses for market research
- Designed market plans for local business
- Promoted and sold worldwide travel packages
- Marketed foreign student internships
- Recruited students and faculty for European seminars

Organization and Management

Managed over 100 government contracts valued at $100,000,000
- Monitored and analyzed contract financial status
- Investigated and resolved contractual issues
- Coordinated team input on program management
- Maintained accuracy of contract closeout procedures
- Performed administrative functions for European seminars

Communication

Served as government liaison
- Advised management on contract progress and changes
- Demonstrated personnel counseling skills
- Wrote detailed closeout procedures for government contracts
- Conducted classroom presentation for seminars

Example 3-1
An Action Résumé

62

Writing the Cover Letter

When you send your résumé to an employer, you will want to include a cover letter that calls attention to the important details in your résumé. In writing your cover letter, you will want to follow some very simple rules:

EMPLOYMENT COVER LETTERS

- Grab the attention of the reader
- Highlight your most important achievements and skills
- Use the "you-attitude"
- Call for action from your reader

Grab the attention of the reader. You want to get the employer to read your cover letter. Be creative, but not gimmicky. Start by naming some of your most important qualifications for the job. For example:

> Strong communication skills, the ability to lead, previous sales experience.
> Do these sound like qualities that you want in your sales representatives?
> If so, you will be interested in seeing me for an interview.

This kind of opening may not work for everyone. It can backfire if you are unable to deliver in the interview. It does grab attention and shows a certain assertiveness and confidence that may help set you apart from all the other candidates.

Highlight your most important achievements and skills. The cover letter should not detail all of your achievements. Your résumé and an interview will provide this kind of detail. The cover letter is where you can tailor the résumé to the job by selecting the key achievements most relevant to the job in question. A good example of this is shown below:

> While earning my college expenses, I developed strong communication
> skills and an ability to manage my time and other resources. As my résumé
> shows, my experience has given me the major qualifications necessary to be
> a successful sales representative for your company.

Use the "you-attitude" in your letter. You need to involve the reader in your letter as soon as possible. Connect your experiences with the needs of the company and the skills of the job. For example:

> Your plans to expand your operations into Mexico fit my career objective.
> I speak fluent Spanish, and I have had experience training non-English-
> speaking employees.

End your letter by calling for some action. The whole purpose of sending an employer your cover letter and résumé is to get an interview. At the end of your letter, you will want to ask the employer to call you or say when you will call for an interview. It is important for you to demonstrate a real desire for the job. Below is an example of a closing from a cover letter for a sales position:

Let's get together to discuss my career opportunities with Software Innovation. I will call you next week to arrange a time for an interview.

Sandy Jenkins is ready to put together her cover letter for the marketing position with Software Innovation. What might this letter look like? Example 3-2 shows a possible approach. What do you think? Are there ways in which this letter could be improved?

Interviewing for the Job

The interview is an important part of the job-seeking process. There are many candidates who look good on paper but do not do well in the interview situation. The interview is often designed to help employers explore gaps from the résumé as well as a candidate's ability to communicate with people. The purpose of most employment interviews is *to give and get information that will help both the interviewer and the interviewee make an effective decision.* A number of tips can help make your interview experience a successful one.

Research the Company and the Job In-Depth. Once you get an interview with the company, it is even more important that you find out as much as possible about the company. Knowing more about the job and the direction of the company becomes very critical. You need to show the interviewer that you have done your homework.

Be Aware of Different Types of Questions. The most common types of questions that you will be asked during an interview are open questions, closed questions, and probes.

Open questions are very broad in scope and help the interviewer find out what is important to the interviewee. Examples of open questions are:

- Tell me a little about yourself.

- Tell me why you decided to major in marketing.

- How did things go for you in your last job?

Closed questions help the interviewer get more specific information and often force a yes-no response from the interviewee. Some examples are:

- Did you enjoy your last job?

- Are you willing to move if the job requires it?

- How soon will you be ready for employment?

Probes help the interviewer get more information by encouraging the interviewee to elaborate more on a particular topic. Probes are neutral and are often no more than an encouraging head nod, or smile. Silence from the interviewer can also encourage further responses from the interviewee. Other examples are:

- Oh?

- Why?

- What makes you think so?

2103 Nevada Avenue
San Jose, CA 95125
April 13, 1993

Mr. Tom Page
Marketing Manager
Software Innovation
10983 Maude Avenue
Mountain View, CA 94043

Dear Mr. Page:

Strong international experience, an ability to do quality marketing research, and previous sales experience. Do these sound like qualities that you want in your marketing research/sales- person? If so, you will be interested in considering me for an interview.

Your interest in finding a person who has extensive marketing research experience fits with my background. I have designed market plans for local businesses abroad using many current marketing analysis techniques. My organization and management skills were developed through the management of over $100,000,000 in government contracts.

Your desire to find a person with international experience in marketing closely matches my career objectives. I definitely want to apply my skills in the international arena. I am fluent in Italian and have worked abroad for a number of years. My experiences abroad have made me very aware of the importance of cultural differences in designing marketing strategies. My unique experiences will help you in your efforts to expand your markets internationally.

Let's get together to discuss the position and possible career opportunities with Software Innovation. I'll call you next week to arrange a time for an interview, or you may reach me at (408) 555-4949.

Cordially,

Sandy Jenkins

Sandy Jenkins

enclosure

Example 3-2
Cover Letter

Become aware of the different types of questions that may be asked at an employment interview, and prepare responses to them. Following are examples of common questions.

The 50 Most Common Interview Questions

The following questions represent those you will likely be asked in an employment interview. *The Endicott Survey* is published periodically by the Placement Center at Northwestern University. The survey is the result of the work of Frank Endicott.

• What are your long-range and short-range goals and objectives? When and why did you establish these goals? How are you preparing yourself to achieve them?

• What specific goals, other than those related to your occupation, have you established for yourself for the next 10 years?

• What do you see yourself doing five years from now?

• What do you really want to do in life?

• What are your long-range career objectives?

• How do you plan to achieve your career goals?

• What are the most important rewards you expect in your career?

• What do you expect to be earning in five years?

• Why did you choose the career for which you are preparing?

• Which is more important to you, the money or the type of job?

• What do you consider to be your greatest strengths and weaknesses?

• How would you describe yourself?

• How do you think a friend or a professor who knows you well would describe you?

• What motivates you to put forth your greatest effort?

• How has your education prepared you for a career?

• Why should I hire you?

• What qualifications do you have that make you think that you will be successful?

• How do you determine or evaluate success?

• What do you think it takes to be successful in a company like ours?

• In what ways do you think you can make a contribution to our company?

• What qualities should a successful manager possess?

• Describe the relationship that should exist between a supervisor and subordinates.

• What two or three accomplishments have given you the most satisfaction? Why?

• Describe your most rewarding college experience.

• If you were hiring a graduate for this position, what qualities would you look for?

• Why did you select your college or university?

66

- What led you to choose your field of major study?

- What academic subjects did you like best? least?

- Do you enjoy doing independent research?

- If you could do so, would you plan your academic study differently?

- What changes would you make in your college or university?

- Do you think that your grades are a good indication of your academic achievement?

- What have you learned from participation in extracurricular activities?

- Do you have plans for continued study? Why did you decide to pursue a graduate degree?

- In what kind of a work environment are you most comfortable?

- How do you work under pressure?

- In what part-time or summer jobs have you been most interested? Why?

- How would you describe the ideal job for you following graduation?

- Why did you decide to seek a position with this company?

- What do you know about our company?

- What two or three things are most important to you in your job?

- Are you seeking employment in a company of a certain size? Why?

- What criteria are you using to evaluate the company for which you hope to work?

- Do you have a geographical preference? Why?

- Will you relocate? Does relocation bother you?

- Are you willing to travel?

- Are you willing to spend at least six months as a trainee?

- Why do you think you might like to live in the community in which our company is located?

- What major problem have you encountered, and how did you deal with it?

- What have you learned from your mistakes?

You can prepare yourself by writing out and practicing your responses to these questions. Find a supportive friend who can act as the interviewer and do some role-playing. This is a good way to get ready for the interview.

Be yourself. Try to act as naturally as possible. Do not act and play a role that is not you. Very few people are able to fool interviewers; employers want people who are comfortable about themselves.

Be professional. You are making a transition from being a student or an employee at another job. This job opportunity requires that you act professional. Do not be overprecise, but be courteous, punctual, organized, and respectful.

Be open. Provide your interviewer with details in your answers to the questions asked. Try not to be vague; give examples to show your experience. This will provide depth and bring out the points that your résumé did not cover.

Turn negatives into positives. Interviewers often point out gaps or weak points in your background. Try to turn the negatives into positives. For example, if you are applying for a sales job and the employer indicates that your résumé shows that you have little actual job experience with personal computer companies, how should you respond?

> **Poor response:** "You're right. I haven't had any experience working in the personal computer business."

> **Better response:** "I think my extensive sales background will more than make up for this. I have been selling for the last five years, and many of the skills that I have developed will help me successfully sell personal computers."

Be honest. Let the interviewer know how you feel about certain things. If something is important to you, it is best to let the employer know right away. If you are unable to relocate, say so immediately rather than wait to be asked to relocate after you have been offered the job.

Relax. If you are well prepared, you should be able to relax. It is normal to be nervous when you first go into the interview. Think before you speak, find a comfortable body position, and maintain it. Remember, the interviewer does not want you to fail or be embarrassed.

Listen. You need to show the interviewer that you are paying attention. Good listening skills are as important as your talking skills. Interviewers often judge your ability to listen. This is a key "people" skill that may be important in the job for which you are interviewing.

Use appropriate nonverbal communication. Eye contact, body posture, tone of voice, and facial expressions are all important aspects to your communication. The following tips may help you in your use of nonverbal communication in the interview:

- **Establish good eye contact.** Look at the interviewer frequently (but avoid staring). Good eye contact suggests to the interviewer that you have confidence and that you are being open and honest.

- **Lean toward the interviewer.** When you are really interested in someone or something, you often sit "on the edge of your seat." Rather than being too casual and leaning back in your chair, sit up and lean toward the interviewer when you are listening and when you speak. Change positions for variety.

- **Give other nonverbal responses.** An occasional "yes" or "uh-huh" is a cue that you are listening. Head nods and smiles will indicate that you are interested in the conversation.

Ask questions. It is essential that you plan some questions to ask the interviewer to show that you have taken the time to prepare yourself.

Following Up After the Interview

A follow-up letter lets the employer know of your continued interest in the position. This is a courteous gesture and good politics; you never know when an interviewer might have a change of heart about hiring you. Your follow-up letter should include:

- An introduction that thanks your interviewer for the time spent;

- A brief message explaining how the interview affected you; and

- A closing that is positive, dominant, and, if you are still interested in working for the company, action-oriented.

A sample follow-up letter is presented on the following page.

2103 Nevada Avenue
San Jose, CA 95125
April 15, 1993

Mr. Tom Page
Marketing Manager
Software Innovation
10983 Maude Avenue
Mountain View, CA 94043

Dear Mr. Page:

Thank you for the time you spent with me during our interview on Tuesday. You increased my interest and desire to work at Software Innovation.

Your marketing research program is particularly interesting to me as it would fit my interests in finding a company with a true desire to do international marketing. I would be most eager to relocate abroad and would welcome the opportunity to use my skills to help keep Software Innovation as competitive as possible.

I look forward to hearing from you.

Sincerely,

Sandy Jenkins

Example 3-3
An Interview Follow-up Letter

70

Exercises

You Write the Response

Here are some typical questions that might be asked in an employment interview. In the space provided, provide an appropriate response based on a job that you are interviewing for.

1. Tell me a little about yourself.

2. Why did you choose to go to _____ University?

3. What did you like best about the jobs you held while going to school?

4. What would you like to be doing five years from now?

5. What do you know about _____ company?

6. What are your greatest strengths for this job?

7. What are your greatest weaknesses for this job?

My Winning Strengths

The following exercise is designed to help you identify your self-perceived strengths. You will be asked in some interviews to talk about them. You may also wish to tailor your cover letter and résumé to bring out these strengths.

Step 1: Put a check beside each word or phrase that describes you, whether you think you are that way all of the time or just part of the time.

Strength Word List

13	busy	08	strong-willed	07	organizer
03	kind	16	motivated	14	tactful
09	artistic	05	admirable	10	committed
04	careful	11	disciplined	15	spontaneous
13	convincing	08	self-reliant	07	commanding
03	friendly	16	persistent	14	tolerant
09	musical	06	neat	10	goal-directed
04	steady	12	caring	15	progressive
13	energetic	02	aware	07	analytical
03	trusting	01	full of ideas	14	faithful
09	gentle	06	accurate	10	authentic
04	loyal	12	helpful	15	adventurous
13	go-getter	02	thinker	05	sharp
03	understanding	01	clever	11	capable
09	charming	06	exact	08	certain
04	stable	12	humorous	16	overcoming
05	distinctive	02	well-informed	05	looked up to
11	perfectionist	01	creative	11	dedicated
08	self-determining	06	orderly	08	courageous
16	pursuing	12	outgoing	16	consistent
05	dignified	02	searching	05	honorable
11	ambitious	01	original	11	productive
08	individualistic	07	fair-minded	08	independent
16	steadfast	14	considerate	16	determined
05	poised	10	fulfilled	05	respected
11	competent	15	flexible	11	efficient
08	confident	16	tireless	13	industrious
03	thoughtful	09	expressive	04	settled
13	persuasive	03	affectionate	09	graceful
04	deliberate	13	influential	03	accepting
09	attractive	04	cautious	13	competitive
03	giving	09	appreciative	04	reliable
07	leader	14	eager	10	growing
15	active	07	planner	14	unselfish
10	self-aware	15	likes new ideas	07	manager
14	cooperative	10	self-directed	15	open-minded
07	forceful	14	dependable	10	adjusted
15	adaptable	06	systematic	12	encouraging
02	curious	01	unique	06	precise

(continued on next page)

12	trustworthy	02	knowledgeable	01	imaginative
06	practical	12	sociable	02	intelligent
01	witty	06	predictable	12	comforting
02	inquiring	01	talented		

Step 2: After checking your strength words, look at the number that goes with each word. Make a tally mark on the tally list at the right side of the page for each time you have checked a word with a given number.

Step 3: Using the numbers from the list below, convert the strengths into strength values.

01 = creativity	1. _____
02 = knowledge	2. _____
03 = relating	3. _____
04 = security	4. _____
05 = prestige	5. _____
06 = order	6. _____
07 = leadership	7. _____
08 = independence	8. _____
09 = beauty	9. _____
10 = self-realization	10. _____
11 = achievement	11. _____
12 = social service	12. _____
13 = economic reward	13. _____
14 = cooperation	14. _____
15 = variety	15. _____
16 = endurance	16. _____

Step 4: Write your five strength values that have the highest number of tally marks in the spaces provided below.

- _____
- _____
- _____
- _____
- _____

Step 5: Identify experiences in your life that have demonstrated these characteristics.

Alternative Exercise: Ask someone who knows you well to complete Step 1 of this exercise. Ask that person to describe you. Discuss your perceptions of yourself and the other person's perceptions of you.

Assignments

Developing the PVA

Each company will prepare a one-page position vacancy announcement (PVA) that identifies available positions; discusses the job responsibilities; lists desired candidate qualifications; describes the company; indicates to whom the letters should be addressed; and contains interview dates, times and sign-up blanks. Once the PVAs are posted in the classroom, students actually sign up for one interview on the PVA. Once sign-ups have been completed, companies retrieve their PVAs to prepare for their interviews. Companies are encouraged to make three to four positions available, appealing to as many business majors in the class as possible. A sample PVA is shown on the next page.

(use this space to work on your PVA)

PVA WORKSHEET

Company Name: _____

Company Description:

Job Title (position #1): _____

Job Responsibilities:

Job Qualifications:

Job Title (position #2): _____

Job Responsibilities:

Job Qualifications:

Job Title (position #3): _____

Job Responsibilities:

Job Qualifications:

Job Title (position #4): _____

Job Responsibilities:

Job Qualifications:

SOFTWARE INNOVATION

NOVA is a San Jose-based software programming company. Our standards of excellence keep us on the leading edge of the software industry. Quality, timeliness, and productivity are essential in NOVA's working environment and the same is looked for from the people we hire. We are fast becoming a leader in employee benefits and career opportunities. We are expanding our product base with the following employment opportunities:

Accounting Clerk

NOVA has an immediate opening for an entry-level accounting clerk. Duties include processing of invoices, research and resolution of unusual transactions, account reconciliations, and month-end close activities. You will also be responsible for interfacing with trade vendors and providing information to local management. Prior accounting experience and/or college-level accounting courses are desirable. Strong communication and organizational skills are required, along with the flexibility necessary for success in a dynamic environment.

Marketing Coordinator

We are looking for a highly skilled and experienced individual to play a major role in developing and maintaining marketing communications and public relations programs. You will oversee the creative and product development processes for a specific product line. Duties will include developing and coordinating related advertising, preparing the annual marketing communications plan, and administering promotional programs. You must have a B.A./B.S. or equivalent in marketing communications, advertising, or journalism with at least two years' progressively responsible experience in marketing or sales.

Sales Manager

We are offering an outstanding opportunity for a sales professional who possesses experience selling in the software industry to manage our area office. The successful individual will possess a B.S. in marketing and/or equivalent experience. You must be self-directed, aggressive, motivated, and eager to work for a rapidly growing company.

Assistant Product
Development Manager

Through the creation of an annual development plan and budget, you will help initiate strategies and programs designed to achieve maximum market penetration of NOVA products. You will help provide functional specifications for product development by formulating and evaluating surveys from user, sales and development groups. While overseeing product documentation and quality assurance testing, you will maintain a level of product and market knowledge that will ensure the completion of development objectives for NOVA products. A B.A./B.S. degree in business administration is necessary.

N★VA
The Brightest Ideas in Program Innovation

Apply in person with résumé at San Jose State University, Business Classroom 312, Monday, January 15, 1993, at the time you have signed up for (below). Please indicate name and position you are applying for.

8:10 a.m.	_____	8:50 a.m.	_____
8:30 a.m.	_____	9:10 a.m.	_____

Developing the Résumé

Prepare a one-page résumé tailored to one of the positions on a company PVA. You are encouraged to apply for a position related to your chosen concentration (accounting, finance, marketing, management, etc.). Treat this assignment as if you were graduating from the university. Use factual information and try to create a model résumé that can be used when you officially graduate. In the space provided below, outline some of the things you will include in your résumé for the PVA and job chosen.

Objective:

Education:

Experience:

Other:

What organizational pattern will you use?
__*Chronological* __*Functional* __*Action* __*Combination*

Explain why:

Developing the Cover Letter

Prepare a one-page cover letter designed to introduce yourself, highlight your résumé, and ask for a job interview.   In the space provided, develop your ideas for the cover letter:

Attract Attention:

Highlight Achievements:

Involve Your Reader:

Use an Action Close:

Conducting the Interview

Each candidate will interview with one company. Candidates will prepare for their interviews with a number of practice exercises designed to help identify their strengths and areas for improvement. Company interviewers will also prepare through exercises provided in the simulation. When candidates are not out at their own interviews, they serve as interviewers for their own companies. Interviews will last 15 minutes. Candidates are encouraged to wear appropriate business attire. In the space provided, your company team can prepare a strategy for conducting the interviews.

Interview Plan

Opening:

Types of Questions:

Information About Job and Company:

Closing:

Providing Feedback

At the conclusion of the interviews, feedback will be given both to the candidates on their résumés, cover letters, and interviews and to the companies on their interviewing strategies. These forms are provided on the next two pages. Record brief notes on each candidate that you interview or observe others interviewing at your company. Share your notes with others in your group. Then, all members of your team should remove the next page from your workbooks. **Each of you should take the responsibility to write the feedback to one of the interviewees and see that it gets to that person.** This feedback is vital to the candidate's professional development. In many cases, this is the only employment interview in which the candidate has ever participated.

NOTES ON CANDIDATES

Candidates' Names

1. _____

   Notes:

2. _____

   Notes:

3. _____

   Notes:

4. _____

   Notes:

5. _____

   Notes:

6. _____

   Notes:

Feedback to Candidate

Name of Candidate: _____

Candidate's Simulation Company: _____
(put feedback sheet in candidate's mailbox when done)

Résumé

Strengths:

Areas for improvement:

Cover Letter

Strengths:

Areas for improvement:

Interview

Strengths:

Areas for improvement:

Company Name: _____
(put feedback sheet in company mailbox when done)

1. What did you like most about the way the company interviewed you?

2. What did you like least about the way the company interviewed you?

3. What suggestions would you make for improvement?

Unit 4

DIRECT COMMUNICATIONS:
WRITING ROUTINE AND GOOD NEWS MESSAGES

Objectives

By successfully completing this unit, you will:

- learn when to write direct messages;
- learn a model showing how to organize direct messages;
- write direct messages;
- edit direct messages; and
- rewrite direct messages.

Case Study

Compuserv plans to hold its annual awards banquet on June 30, and Marilyn Wu has been assigned to locate an appropriate site. This is a very important event at Compuserv, and it must be handled well. Marilyn has heard good things about The Safari Room, but she needs to know if it will be able to accommodate the party on that evening. Compuserv plans for about 250 people to attend. Marilyn would like a no-host cocktail bar to be set up one hour before the dinner begins at 7 p.m. She wants to know if a stage and microphones can be set up for after-dinner ceremonies. She has arranged for a speaker and presentation of awards. She wants a special table for honored guests. She wants to know how the restaurant would like to handle payment for all of this.

Writing Good News and Routine Messages

Most of the messages you write in business fall into the "routine" category. For convenience, we often refer to messages as "good news" and "bad news"; remember, however, that good news includes routine messages. You should also consider whether the message is being sent inside or outside the organization and whether you are initiating an interaction or responding to someone else's message.

	INITIATING	RESPONDING
INSIDE ORGANIZATION	• Direct inquiries (information requests, reports, etc.) • Announcements (meetings, policy changes, etc.) • Appreciation, congratulations	• Replies to inquiries (information requests, reports) • Acknowledgments (information received, action taken)
OUTSIDE ORGANIZATION	• Orders to suppliers • Direct inquiries (products, services, personnel, etc.) • Appreciation, congratulations • Claim adjustment requests • Credit requests	• Replies to inquiries • Acknowledgments applications, requests, orders) • Claim adjustments granted • Credit granted

Source: John W. Baird and James B. Stull, *Business Communication: Strategies and Solutions*, New York: McGraw-Hill, 1983, p. 127.

Figure 4-1
Types of Good News and Routine Messages

Many of us would probably use the telephone to arrange a banquet or to handle other routine messages; for various reasons, however, you may wish to put the message in writing. Look at Marilyn Wu's first draft of her letter to The Safari Room (Example 4-1). Has she organized her message so that it is easy to understand? Is her purpose clear? Perhaps it is if the reader has time to study it. But, during the business day, most people are busy and would prefer a more direct approach that is easier to scan. Use the space below to critique her letter.

How would you improve Marilyn's first draft?

COMPUSERV

1256 Semiconductor Drive, Silicon Valley, CA   90000   (408) 555-5289
Serving Silicon Valley's supply needs since 1960

November 15, 1993

Mr. Marvin Melvin
Banquet Coordinator
The Safari Room
One Boardwalk
Alviso, CA 95002

Dear Mr. Melvin:

We have heard great things about The Safari Room. Some of our employees have eaten there, and they said that it might be a good place to hold a banquet. Every year Compuserv honors its best employees with an awards banquet. This is a major event for our company, and we want it to be done right. Normally, we like to have a special table for our honored guests. Also, a microphone and a stage would be helpful for our ceremonies. A no-host cocktail bar should be set up one hour before dinner begins. The dinner is scheduled for 7 p.m. on June 30, 1994. We expect about 250 people to attend that evening. Can you also send me information on how you would like to handle the financial arrangements for this?

I look forward to hearing from you soon.

Sincerely,

Marilyn Wu

Marilyn Wu, Administrative Assistant
Personnel Department

Example 4-1
A Poorly Written Routine Request

Characteristics of Good News and Routine Messages

Good news and routine messages should be clear and concise. The clear and concise presentation of accurate information is essential to the success of good news and, particularly, routine messages. Routine messages are neither special nor unique. Since managers send and receive so many routine messages, clarity and conciseness are particularly important in facilitating their routine processing.

Good news and routine messages sent within the company follow memo format. Memos are less formal and are most appropriate among employees of the same company. They do not require a postal system mailing address, a salutation, or a complimentary close.

Good news and routine messages sent outside the company follow letter format. Letters are more formal and are most appropriate for communicating messages outside the company. To maintain the proper company image, writers should learn and use an acceptable letter style.

Good news and routine messages should not appear too routine. While many routine and favorable messages are relatively easy to write, you should be careful about being too concise. Whenever possible, you should try to make your letter personal. Goodwill and diplomacy are of paramount importance. With the widespread use of computerized and form letters, people are becoming suspect of many messages, even when their names are sprinkled in at strategic places.

Good news and routine messages that are responses may be more concise than those that initiate interactions. Communications that answer a previous message (replies to inquiries, requests, or acknowledgments) often require less explanation or clarification than those intended to direct or inform for the first time. Often, the mere mention of a previous message creates a frame of reference. You should avoid redundancy or laboring an issue when you can; yet, if some time has elapsed between messages, you may wish to refresh the reader's memory.

Good news and routine messages, by their very nature, communicate the importance of a quick response. Most good news and routine messages imply that a quick response is desirable. Companies like to know that an order has been received; people like to know that their questions are being answered.

Companies need information to make decisions. The more quickly you respond, the more positive your image will be. This positive image will help promote credible professional relationships within your company and with other organizations. Slow responses often lead to lost business. Consider the following model for good news and routine messages.

MODEL FOR GOOD NEWS
AND ROUTINE MESSAGES

- **Start with the main point.**
- **Follow with any necessary details.**
- **End on a positive, friendly note.**

Note that the purpose of the message, the main point, is presented right away. This is why we call this type of message *direct*. Let's look at the components of the model and the rationale behind each.

Start with the main point. When you can communicate what your reader wants to hear, you do not need any introductory comments. Get to the good news or main point as quickly as possible. This creates a very positive impression.

Follow with any necessary details. Once the good news or routine communication has opened with the main point, the next step is to provide the appropriate explanation. One important question is, "How much does my reader need to know to understand my message?" Try to see it from your reader's point of view.

End on a positive, friendly note. Business messages should typically end on a positive, friendly note. To end a message without an expression of goodwill can result in negative reactions from the reader. Create a closing that blends well with the content and tone of the accompanying message.

Having covered these points, let's now analyze the letter written by Marilyn Wu. Has she been direct? Does Mr. Melvin know right away what she wants? Should he have to read through the letter to figure out what she wants? Has she organized her message so that Mr. Melvin can determine what special arrangements she needs? Is the letter easy to scan?

What can you say now about Marilyn's letter?

COMPUSERV

1256 Semiconductor Drive, Silicon Valley, CA   90000 (408) 555-5289
Serving Silicon Valley's supply needs since 1960

November 15, 1993

Mr. Marvin Melvin
Banquet Coordinator
The Safari Room
One Boardwalk
Alviso, CA 95002

Dear Mr. Melvin:

Direct request Can The Safari Room accommodate 250 people for a banquet on June 30? If so, can you also provide:

- a no-host cocktail bar at 6 p.m.
- dinner at 7 p.m.

Details
- a stage and microphone and
- a special table for honored guests?

Compuserv plans to hold its annual awards banquet that evening. The Safari Room is the first choice for this very special occasion.

Positive/ friendly close Also, please send information on how The Safari Room prefers to handle payment for such an event. I look forward to hearing from you soon.

Sincerely,

Marilyn Wu

Marilyn Wu, Administrative Assistant
Personnel Department

Example 4-2
A Routine Message

Now, let's consider various types of routine and good news messages to determine their content; then we'll look at an example of how one of these messages might actually be written.

Congratulations

You may wish to congratulate one of your officemates for getting promoted, for winning an award, for being accepted into a graduate program, or for any other reason. Try to follow this simple model.

CONGRATULATIONS

- Congratulate the individual.
- Praise the individual.
- Provide any details, if necessary.
- Offer your best wishes and support.

Notes:

Advanced Software

5858 Industrial Parkway, Silicon Valley, CA 95000 (408) 555-9821

June 28, 1991

Ms. Carolyn Paeva
5634 Maiden Lane
Englewood Cliffs, NJ 07632

Dear Carolyn:

Congratulations   Congratulations! You have been selected as Advanced Software's new manager of educational software.

Praise   After reviewing over one hundred qualified candidates, our selection committee found you best suited for the position.

Details   Please plan to start on August 1. You will report to Kenneth Walden, vice president of software development. During your first two days, plan to attend several meetings and seminars to familiarize yourself with more of our key people and policies.

Support   Please call me at any time when I can assist you. You can count on my support.

Sincerely,

Dana Solari
Chair, Search Committee

DS/jbs

Example 4-3
A Congratulations Letter

Announcement

Frequently, you must announce a meeting or event, the hiring of a new manager or employee, or a new policy. Here's a model that works.

ANNOUNCEMENT

- State the announcement in the first sentence.
- Show the importance of the announcement to the other person.
- Provide the necessary details.
- Express goodwill and support.

Tri-County Supply Company

MEMO

TO: Friends in the Word Processing Pool   October 28, 1991

FROM: Sandy Birch, Social Committee *S.B.*

RE: Friday's Festivities

Announcement	You are invited to a company party on Friday at 3 p.m. in the cafeteria.
Relationship to receiver	You will have an opportunity to express your appreciation to Dan Burns and Lennie Welch. Dan and Lennie are retiring after 25 years with the company.
Details	The party is a surprise. Please bring a gag gift and be prepared to say something appropriately funny as we roast both Dan and Lennie. For those of you who would like to contribute toward a more serious gift for both of them, please see Stacey Zeal. She also has farewell cards you can sign.
Goodwill/ support	Please plan to attend this fun event, as we all want to wish our two long-time, good friends the best of luck.

Example 4-4
An Announcement Memorandum

Placing an Order

Most of the time you want to place an order, you will telephone it to the supplier or fill out an order form or purchase requisition. However, you should know how to write an order letter. It's as simple as this.

PLACING AN ORDER

- State what you want.
- Specify any payment preferences.
- Express your expectations about delivery date and acknowledgement.

Notes:

Joshua Jacob and Associates

4500 Industrial Parkway, Suite 100, Silicon Valley, CA 95000 (408) 555-6565

Silicon Valley's Leader in Organizational Development   *Training, Consulting, Image Building*

January 15, 1992

Gulf Publishing Company
Book Division
P. O. Box 2608
Houston, TX 77252

RE: Book Request

General
request

Please send 250 copies of *Managing Cultural Differences* by Harris and Moran.

Payment
preferences

Enclosed is purchase order #243546, reflecting our normal 20 percent discount and no shipping or handling charges.

Expectations

We are planning to use the books in our training seminars in March. Please let us know how soon we can expect delivery. Thanks.

JOSHUA JACOB AND ASSOCIATES

Maria Villareal

Maria Villareal
Office Manager

MV/jbs

Example 4-5
An Order Letter

Acknowledging an Order

Many companies follow the policy of letting a customer know that an order has been received, particularly when filling the order and shipping it might take some time. Try using this model.

ACKNOWLEDGING AN ORDER

- State that the order has been received (and filled, if appropriate).
- Specify details about shipping, billing, etc.
- Thank the customer and encourage future business.

Notes:

Valley T-Shirt Company
25 First Street, Silicon Valley, CA
(408) 555-8578

April 25, 1992

Mr. Devon McIntyre
American Supply Company
54653 South Park Drive
Silicon Valley, CA 95000

Dear Mr. McIntyre:

Acknowledge order   Your order for 2,000 T-shirts has been received. Production is scheduled for next week.

Describe terms   You can expect delivery by May 15. Your account will be billed, and you will receive a 10 percent good customer discount.

Thanks Repeat business   Thank you for relying on Valley T-Shirt for your special orders. Please call again when we can be of service to you.

Sincerely,

Carl Cook

Carl Cook
Customer Service

CC/jbs

Example 4-6
An Acknowledgment Letter

Direct Inquiries

You will often need to request information on people, products, services, etc. Once you determine your overall purpose for the message, you may use the following model.

DIRECT INQUIRY

- Ask your major question.
- Clarify with sub-requests or sub-questions.
- Provide explanation where necessary.
- End on a positive, friendly note.

Notes:

Advanced Electronics
Two Melbourne Place
Silicon Valley, CA 95000

We're the ones to watch   (408) 555-3764

June 10, 1992

Dr. Reneé Pinot
The Right Image
Two Plaza Mall
Silicon Valley, CA 95000

Dear Dr. Pinot:

Direct inquiry

Are you available to conduct a seminar on quality circles any time in August?

Advanced Electronics has identified specific needs for this type of training. Can you tailor your training to deal with the following types of situations:

Sub-questions

- engineers with no management training
- managers with little technical knowledge
- employees who represent several cultures?

Explanation

Quality circles should increase productivity, decrease down time and improve overall morale. Terry Downs praises your program and the impact it had on Beta, Inc.

Positive close

Please let me know soon about your availability so that we can make the necessary arrangements.

Cordially,

Paula Johns
Training Manager

PJ:jbs

Example 4-7
A Direct Inquiry Letter

99

Requesting Credit

Often, when you want a company to grant you credit, you complete a detailed application form. Perhaps, in many cases, you would telephone the company or drop by the credit office of a company to pick up the application form. However, if you decided to write a letter to request credit, you could try the following approach.

REQUESTING CREDIT

- Ask for credit or a charge account.
- Provide a history of residence, employment, other credit, etc.
- End on a positive, confident note.

Notes:

Futronics, Inc.

1123 Twenty-fifth Avenue
Silicon Valley, CA 95000
(408) 555-7890

January 23, 1992

Everett Oil Products
56342 Lakeshore Drive
San Francisco, CA 94132

Request   Please open a credit card account in the name of Futronics, Inc.

Details   Futronics has been a leading electronic parts supplier in Silicon
Valley since 1960. Many employees drive company vehicles and
have frequent need to purchase gasoline and oil. Futronics has
just authorized individual credit cards for its designated
employees. Futronics has made similar arrangements with
Computerworld and Software Plus. Please feel free to contact
them if you would like to check on Futronics' credit history.

Positive   Futronics looks forward to establishing a long-term relationship
close   with Everett Oil Products.

FUTRONICS, INC.

Xavier Remy

Xavier Remy
Purchasing Manager

XR:jbs

Example 4-8
Request for Credit

Granting Credit

When you have decided to grant credit to a customer, here is how you might deliver the good news.

GRANTING CREDIT

- State that the credit has been granted.
- Compliment the person on being accepted.
- Explain the details of the credit agreement.
- Thank the customer, and encourage a long-term relationship.

Notes:

Computer   Galaxy   ☆ ☆ ☆ ☆   A Star in Silicon Valley

2 Fashion Plaza Mall, Silicon Valley, CA 95000 (408) 555-4565

June 11, 1992

Mr. Dominic Guido
1525 Santa Teresa Court
Silicon Valley, CA 95000

Dear Mr. Guido:

Credit granted	Congratulations! Your application for a charge account with Computer Galaxy has been approved.
Compliment	Your excellent credit and employment history easily qualified you for our preferred customer status. Only about 10 percent of our customers earn this.
Details	As a preferred customer, you have 30 days to pay off your balance each month, with a 10-day grace period. You are also given advanced notice of all sales and an invitation to purchase any products before they become available to the general public.
Thanks/ relationship	Thank you for shopping at Computer Galaxy. We look forward to serving all of your computer needs.

Sincerely,

Delia Grande

Delia Grande
Assistant Manager
Credit Department

Example 4-9
Credit Acknowledgment Letter

103

Requesting a Claim Adjustment

When you need to have your account adjusted, when you need a product serviced or replaced because of a defect covered by a warranty, and in similar types of circumstances, treat the situation as a positive request.

REQUESTING A CLAIM ADJUSTMENT

- State your request.
- Describe the product in detail.
- Explain why you are requesting action.
- Express your expectation of a positive outcome.
- Thank the reader for handling your request.

Notes:

Dos Tequis

23-10 Avenida de la Reforma, Ensenada, Mexico
Telephone   011-52-667-567-9876

July 15, 1992

Mr. Jim McDonald
Accounts Supervisor
Component Warehouse
6000 Silicon Valley Blvd.
Silicon Valley, CA 95000

Dear Jim:

Request   Please credit our account for $750 for the latest shipment of printed circuit boards that we are returning.

Describe   The SuperXL boards were included with our order for XL503 boards. Currently, we have an excess of SuperXL boards, and we **Explain**   need the warehouse space for our other inventory.

Confidence   I'll let you know when we need another order of SuperXL .
Thanks   boards. Thanks for taking care of this.

Cordially,

Ernesto Chavez

Ernesto Chavez
Receiving Supervisor

EC/jbs

Example 4-10
Claim Adjustment Request

Adjusting a Claim

When you decide to honor the request of a customer by adjusting a claim, treat it as good news.

ADJUSTING A CLAIM

- State that the request is being honored.
- Make the customer feel correct in making the claim.
- Explain how the claim improves future products or services.
- Encourage further business.
- Thank the customer for the request.

Notes:

Component Warehouse
6000 Silicon Valley Blvd.
Silicon Valley, CA 95000
(408) 555-9878

July 20, 1993

Sr. Ernesto Chavez
Dos Tequis
23-10 Avenida de la Reforma
Ensenada, Mexico

Dear Ernesto:

Request honored

Your account has been credited for $750 for the shipment of the SuperXL boards that you returned.

Benefit Shown

With the success of your XL503, you must need all the space you can get to store its boards. We should investigate starting a just-in-time inventory program at Dos Tequis. This will save you a great deal of money in inventory holding costs.

Further business Thanks

Please call me any time to assist you with your supply needs, and thank you for letting me help you with your most recent order.

Cordially,

Jim McDonald
Accounts Supervisor

JM/jbs

Example 4-11
Adjustment Letter

107

References and Recommendations

You will frequently be asked to serve as a reference for someone and to write a letter of recommendation. Employers want to know if the person is a self-starter, a leader, a decision maker. Is the person cooperative, motivated, trustworthy, responsible, organized, reliable? Does the person have a good attitude, good communication skills? You might follow a model similar to this, being sure to specify the person's strengths and, if necessary, areas for improvement.

LETTER OF RECOMMENDATION

- Express your pleasure in serving as a reference.
- Explain how you know the individual.
- Provide specific details on the person's abilities and character.
- Assure the reader of your confidence in the candidate.
- Offer to provide additional information.

Notes:

Zebra Manufacturing

1000 Recreational Park Drive, Silicon Valley, CA 95000 (408) 555-1111

July 8, 1993

Mr. William Johnson
Personnel Manager
Canary Computer Center
23 Vincent Place
Silicon Valley, CA 95000

Dear Mr. Johnson:

Pleasure   Ms. Leslie Wirth has applied for the marketing and sales representative position at Canary. It is a pleasure to serve as a reference for her.

Relationship   Leslie worked for Zebra for three years while she was attending college. She started out as a receptionist and quickly earned her current position as customer service representative. She was recognized for her outstanding communication skills and ability to work with the public.

Details   Leslie organizes projects so that they are completed with efficiency; she manages her time well. During her three years at Zebra, Leslie developed a customer wellness program, with the purpose of contacting new owners of Zebra products to assure them that they had made a wise choice. Zebra sales representatives have remarked that she is responsible for many repeat business customers.

We would like Leslie to stay on here and work for us as a sales representative, but she has a true interest in Canary's plans to move into the Eastern European market. She speaks German and Russian fluently.

Confidence   Leslie is a rising star who will stand out in any company fortunate enough to attract and hire her. I'm sure you will agree once you see what she is capable of achieving.

Example 4-12
Letter of Recommendation

William Johnson
July 8, 1993
Page 2

Offer   Please call on me if I can provide further information.
You have my strongest recommendation for Leslie Wirth.

Sincerely,

Thurmon Kiely
Sales Manager

TK:jbs

Example 4-12
Letter of Recommendation
(two-page letter format)

Exercises:

The Opening Line

For each of the following situations, write the first sentence of a letter or memorandum you would send.

1. Tell a candidate for the position of accounting manager that she has been selected for that job.

2. Announce to the accounting department that Jackie Smith is the new accounting manager.

3. Place an order for 10,000 SC40 machine bearings for Wilson generators.

4. Acknowledge that you have received and filled the order for 10,000 SC40 machine bearings for Wilson generators.

5. Ask a C.P.A. firm if it is still advisable to save receipts for medical expenses, even though you do not have enough expenses to qualify for a deduction.

6. Request that a retailer open an account for you and send you a credit card.

7. Tell a customer that your company has opened an account in her name and that a credit card is being sent to her.

8. Ask that your company be given credit or replacement for 500 reams of damaged stationery that you received.

9. Respond that you have granted your customer credit for 500 reams of damaged stationery returned to you.

Editing a Memorandum

The following memorandum was written by students to illustrate a message that is wordy and unclear. Read it, determine its purpose, edit it, and rewrite it.

November 20, 1991

To: All Factory and Office Employees

From: J. B. Windy, Personnel Manager

Subject: Holiday Vacation

It has come to my attention that many of you have been asking about a vacation during the holiday season. This memorandum is in answer to these questions that you have been asking.

As a matter of fact, you will be happy and glad that according to our company policy established on this year, which may be true for only this year, there will be a holiday break during the Christmas season of eight days, including weekends, when everything is closed for all of the employees in the factory as well as all of those in the offices. These eight days begin at the end of the regular working day on December 23, which is, as you know, at 4 p.m., and extends to January 2 to the regular opening hour of 8 a.m.

As I said, we will all be on vacation then. And the best part of it is that the regular pay will continue, for all the time of the vacation, except of course for the weekends, when you aren't paid anyway, unless you count what you earn during the week as being spread over the weekends. And you still get your regular vacation.

Your company is grateful and appreciative of your work during the preceding and past year. As a kind of thank you and bonus, we are making this time off available. Have a happy holiday season. Don't hesitate to call me if you have any questions.

Homework Problems

Manufacturing Company

Manufacturing Company to Assembly Company Your company has decided to make some personnel changes in the management of your assembly plant in Mexico. The software development division can show greater profits with some reorganization because of your latest venture—the development of software programs in Spanish for the Mexican market. Your company plans to relocate three of its staff to help the assembly company's vice president of software development. The personnel you are sending are Margaret O'Brien, manager of software development; Carla Wilkes, assistant manager of business software development; and Charles Williams, assistant manager of educational software development. Write a letter to your counterpart in the assembly company to announce this news.

Manufacturing Company to Supply Company Many large companies have previously relied on mainframe computers to process information. Personal computer (PC) networks have begun to replace mainframes in many of those companies. Many of the companies that have switched to PC networks report that people no longer wait in lines to use the mainframes and that PCs are less expensive and faster. With this change in the industry comes a need for more supplies from your supply distribution company. Your analysts anticipate a 5 percent increase in demand for your XL503. Write a letter to your counterpart in the supply company to request that they be prepared to supply your assembly company with the necessary parts.

Manufacturing Company to Software Company Your company has spent the past several years promoting an internal "wellness" program encouraging healthy living to its employees. The program encourages better eating habits and regular exercise and discourages cigarette smoking and alcohol and drug abuse. Company medical costs for the last year were $85.6 million, up 10 percent from the previous year. The rest of the industry experienced a 20 percent increase. Your latest study indicates that only 18 percent of your employees smoke; five years ago, over 30 percent of your employees smoked. The same study also showed a 30 percent increase in the use of your company's exercise facility and an increase in healthier foods purchased at the company cafeteria. A cholesterol screening program led to an 8.7 percent decrease in overall cholesterol levels among your employees. Your company began marketing this program to other companies six months ago. Write to your counterpart in the software company, announcing this program. Encourage your counterpart to discuss this program within the software company. Make yourself available for further information or a presentation to the software company.

Manufacturing Company to Retail Company Your company has been able to reduce production costs on the XL503; the suggested retail price of the computer will now be cut 15.2 percent to $2,150. Many of the savings have come from a new lightweight, inexpensive material used in the actual body of the computer. Your management believes that both the lowered price and ease of carrying will make this product even more attractive and successful. You are also planning to offer a carrying case, an updated user-friendly tutorial, and a 100-diskette file storage system with the purchase of the computer. Write to your counterpart in the retail company to announce this information about your product.

Manufacturing Company to Public Relations Company Your company has decided to move part of its research and development division (R & D) to Singapore. Singapore is attracting R & D, automation, and technology in an effort to become Southeast Asia's center of technology. Singapore provides low-cost labor, a huge availability of electronic components and related supplies, a strategic location for communication with and transportation to other Asian markets, political stability, and a population thirsting to be educated as researchers, software engineers, and biotechnology specialists. Several large U.S. manufacturers have moved their R & D facilities to Singapore because of the tax breaks offered by the Singapore government. This will also be a great opportunity for your company to move into the Asian computer user market. Write to your counterpart in the public relations company, announcing your plans to move part of your operation to Singapore; you might also ask how the public relations company plans to use this information to promote your company in an appropriate manner.

Assembly Company

Assembly Company to Manufacturing Company Your plant is managed primarily by U.S. managers. They have worked in Mexico for some time and have expressed interest in cross-cultural training to increase their sensitivity to their Mexican employees. They are aware that their use of the Spanish language and their understanding of the Mexican culture could be better. Your parent company in the United States has encouraged you to consider training in the past, and has indicated that several good trainers in Silicon Valley are interested in conducting the training. Write a letter to your counterpart in the manufacturing company to indicate your needs and to request information on this type of training program.

Assembly Company to Supply Company Your company has just settled a deal with Serendipity Printers. Serendipity has decided to focus more of its attention on research and development and to have your company assemble all of its printers. It is the largest printer manufacturer in the world, which means a considerable increase in production for your company. You will need to hire more employees, add to and modify the equipment in your plant, and maintain a new inventory line. Write to your counterpart in the supply company, announcing this new venture and that your future purchase orders will include assembly parts for Serendipity printers. Request a price list for Serendipity's parts and supplies.

Assembly Company to Software Company Your company's management and your parent company's management have negotiated with German manufacturers, and you plan to open an assembly plant in Eisenach, Germany. Recent events in Europe have encouraged this venture. However, it will require some additional research and planning. You have been asked to contact your counterpart in the software company to announce this news and to find out what software exists that has been written in German and the other languages in these new markets.

Assembly Company to Retail Company Your company has designed and developed a "fault tolerant" computer. This type of computer is often used by banks, securities companies and telecommunications firms. It is built with duplicate circuits to ensure the system's operation when a component fails. It does not compete with the XL503; in fact, it is compatible. PC users can actually hook up to this central computer. Write a letter to your counterpart in the retail company announcing this new product and its compatibility with the XL503. Your management believes that this will result in more business for the XL503.

Assembly Company to Public Relations Company Recent studies by the Mexican government identified 15 plants that were found to be in violation of Mexico's pollution regulations. According to Mexico's state-run news agency, *Notimex*, plants have been closed temporarily for discharging untreated waste water into open ravines and for dumping fuels into the drainage system. Waste water from other firms has damaged 14 cooperative farms. Another company was closed for dumping harmful zinc and lead residues into a local river. This has caused concern in your area. Your company was found not to be in violation of any pollution standards. In fact, your company was praised by the investigators as a leader in environmental awareness and action. Your management believes that this positive information should be publicized. Write to your counterpart in the public relations company requesting publicity on your company's environmental conscientiousness.

Supply Company

Supply Company to Manufacturing Company Your company recently negotiated with a Japanese computer chip manufacturer to trade one of your warehouses and an assembly line for the Japanese company's computer chip expertise. Your management believes that by being able to offer a superior computer chip, you will capture a significant portion of the market. The manufacturer of the XL503 has been interested in improved chips and will be excited to hear the news. Write to your counterpart in the manufacturing company to announce this recent acquisition.

Supply Company to Assembly Company Your management recently decided to include instructions written in Spanish with all shipments sent to the assembly plant in Mexico. Your counterpart has commented on several occasions that each time technology is updated, someone has to translate the instructions for the Mexican assembly workers. Since so many of your employees in Silicon Valley are bilingual and some are even from the same city in which the assembly company is located, your staff is confident that the newly translated instructions will be understood and in the proper dialect for that region. It has also been suggested that this could result in a slight increase in productivity. Write to your counterpart in the assembly company to announce this news.

Supply Company to Software Company Your company has been providing just-in-time delivery for your customers; however, in order to do this, your company has had to maintain a large inventory. Basically, you have been helping your customers save on inventory holding costs, but your inventory holding costs have been high. You plan to begin a just-in-time inventory program for your company; to do this, you will need to know the projected supplies requirements from your customers for the next quarter. If you can determine when you will need certain quantities of supplies to meet your customers' needs, you will be able to order those supplies, process them through your company, and pass along some of your savings from reduced overhead to your customers. Write to your counterpart in the software company to find out how much of which types of supplies will be needed.

Supply Company to Retail Company A Japanese semiconductor maker recently licensed its technology to your company, allowing your company to enter a small, rapidly growing segment of the semiconductor market. Now, your company will be able to produce its own computer chips and supply its customers with high quality chips at competitive prices. Many retail stores order their replacement parts from your company and will be happy about the higher quality of the chips. Write to your counterpart in the retail company to announce this news.

Supply Company to Public Relations Company Your company has experienced a decline in sales over the past year because of increased competition in Silicon Valley. You wish to reposition your company in the supply market, but before you commit to further advertising, you want a market research study conducted. You want to know the similarities and differences in products and services between your company and your competitors. You also want to know how current and prospective customers perceive your company, including their likes and dislikes. Write a letter to your counterpart in the public relations company, requesting that such a study be conducted.

115

Software Company

Software Company to Manufacturing Company Your company has just completed a software product on compact discs, designed to be marketed with the XL503. The product is called *Knowledgeware*. It is a complete encyclopedia with text, sound, and pictures. It contains all of the information of a 26-volume encyclopedia, with 15,000 pictures, 5,800 maps and charts (allowing users to "travel" to various spots on the globe), and 60 minutes of sound (music, famous speeches, etc.). The XL503 has a built-in drive that can read the compact discs. Write to your counterpart in the manufacturing company, announcing this exciting new software.

Software Company to Assembly Company In order for your company to continue to develop software products, your technicians need to test products on the hardware for which they have been designed. This requires constant upgrading of computers. Your company has been designing software for multi-user computers, networks that can provide computing power to dozens of people at once. The assembly company has begun production of these computers, and you would like one for your research and development staff. Write to your counterpart in the assembly company, requesting one of these computers. You realize that they cost about $45,000 each, and would like one either on loan or purchased at a significant discount, as you have a cooperative relationship with the assembly company.

Software Company to Supply Company Your company has just unveiled an "active document" software that allows the user to update documents in and get data from other computers automatically. With the proper authorization, the user accesses a network and updates all documents that are affected by a transaction. Your management believes that this will be a great advantage to all users. For example, your supply company could know when to send a just-in-time order to the assembly company, notify the manufacturing company, update accounts receivable and sales journals and record the information to many other documents with just one entry. Write to your counterpart in the supply company, announcing the unveiling of this new software.

Software Company to Retail Company Your company has just set up a 24-hour "help line" for software users who need assistance. Previously, users called the retail stores for assistance with either software or hardware. Often, however, the retail service centers must call your company, try to relate the customer's problem to your staff, and then contact the customer with your staff's suggestions. Sometimes, this involves multiple calls. Your management believes that this new service will strengthen your relationship with retailers and customers and decrease the number of calls to the stores' service centers, allowing their technicians to focus on repair and maintenance. Customers can talk directly with your company's experts. Your help line's telephone number is 1-800-SOFTFIX. Write to your counterpart in the retail company to announce this new service.

Software Company to Public Relations Company Your company has just developed a new software program that combines word processing and spreadsheet capabilities in one package. The program is called *Edutech*, and is targeted toward the education market. Your software development personnel have spent over two years and thousands of dollars on *Edutech*; now they want to know how it will be received by the public. Write to your counterpart in the public relations company and ask that a feasibility study be conducted for you.

Retail Company

Retail Company to Manufacturing Company About two months ago, you entered into a cooperative agreement with the manufacturer of the XL503 and your public relations company

116

to determine the market for an innovative product, the notepad computer. These small computers allow the user to write information on an electronic pad rather than type in figures on a keyboard. The computer is compatible with the XL503 operating system (as well as with some of the manufacturing company's competitors' models). While these notepad computers will initially retail for about $3,000 each, competition will drive the price down. Projections are that this year the market demand for the computer will be about 20,000 units; in five years, the estimate reaches 3.5 million units. Some concern was expressed over whether the machines could actually decipher different people's handwriting. Write to your counterpart in the manufacturing company to report the findings on market demand and to request 1,000 units to be sold in your chain of stores.

Retail Company to Assembly Company You order the XL503 directly from the assembly company. You have had an unusually large request for computers from your stores; the demand has been high because of heavy advertising and testimonials to the success of the computer. You believe that a great deal of the manufacturing company's success may be attributed to the quality control efforts at the assembly company. Write to your counterpart in the assembly company to say thanks and to give praise for a job well done.

Retail Company to Supply Company Your service department is expanding due to the introduction of the XL503 computer. You are a major distributor of this product and one of the few service centers in the area. You wish to keep a substantial supplies inventory to expedite service to your retail customers. Two items you replace most often are the wiring harness (XL503-H22) and the wiring harness reenforcing shield (XL503-H23). You believe that an order of 500 of each item will meet your needs for a while. Write to your counterpart in the supply company to order these items.

Retail Company to Software Company You recently learned that the software company has developed a new program to keep track of inventory, both at the individual store level and at headquarters. This program, *Invenet*, monitors the inventory level of all products by model, size, color, and other important characteristics; orders supplies for your service centers; and tells you immediately if what you need is available at one of your other stores. You would like brochures, price lists, discount policies, and any other information that might help you and your staff consider purchasing such a program. Please write to your counterpart in the software company, requesting this information.

Retail Company to Public Relations Company Your company recently decided to offer its own credit card. Retail customers may now charge their purchases on your store's card and pay 18 percent interest annually. You allow a 30-day grace period on purchases. After 60 days, customers will pay a small late charge. This card does not require a membership fee, which many other credit card companies charge. Credit card customers receive discounts on certain items and advanced notice of sales to provide an incentive to purchase computers and computer products at your store. Write to your counterpart at the public relations company, requesting that they prepare an advertising campaign to announce this news.

Public Relations Company

Public Relations Company to Manufacturing Company You recently learned that the manufacturer of the XL503 computer has just completed designing a "ternary chording" keyboard. This revolutionary keyboard splits in the middle and resembles an open book, face down. It allows users to type with palms facing each other, causing less strain than do flat keyboards. The keyboard has only eight keys, with three positions each (forward, back, and neutral). The operator can generate 64 characters. Your management staff has asked you to write to the manufacturer to inquire about the product and, in particular, to offer your marketing research services. Write to your counterpart in the manufacturing company.

Public Relations Company to Assembly Company Your president, vice presidents, and their support staff plan to relocate from the company's Silicon Valley location to Chula Vista, a small town in southern California, near the U.S.-Mexico border. Following an industrial trend, your leaders made this move to reduce overhead in the more expensive headquarters in Silicon Valley and to take advantage of communication technology that allows this type of move. This move will also allow more independent decision making at both locations. A side benefit is that you are closer to your assembly company account in Mexico. Write to your counterpart in the assembly company to announce this move. Your new address will be 123 Avenida de las Pulgas, Chula Vista, CA 92012.

Public Relations Company to Supply Company Your supply account has recently been recognized by the computer industry as the most dependable supplier in the United States. The company's just-in-time program and its nationwide 24-hour delivery guarantee have driven the company beyond its competition. The quality of the parts delivered has reached an all-time high. Sales have doubled in one year. The company's personnel are regarded as the "friendliest anywhere." Your company has contributed to the supply company's success. You have created advertisements, marketing plans, and general public announcements that you regard as truly excellent. However, you realize that the true talent lies in the individuals responsible for leadership in the supply company. Write to your counterpart in the supply company, offering your congratulations and continued support.

Public Relations Company to Software Company Your company has decided to branch out, with satellite offices in three other locations across the country. In order for all account managers to have access to common data, you will need software programs that link your branches together. Write to your counterpart in the software company, requesting assistance in setting up such a network system.

Public Relations Company to Retail Company You have decided to assign Sarah Williams to manage your retail account. Sarah is fresh out of one of the leading advertising graduate programs in the country, having earned her M.A. from Northwestern University. She specializes in magazine advertising. She completed an internship with the Chicago branch of BBDO, a large, prestigious advertising firm. Sarah will work under the supervision of your vice president of retail accounts. Write to your counterpart in the retail company, announcing this change.

...*about the simulation.*.. In Unit 5 you will learn about using indirect communications, primarily sending bad or negative messages and persuasive appeals. You will send indirect messages to your counterparts in other companies. Your counterparts may choose to respond through self-initiated assignments (SIAs). The SIAs should also be indirect messages.

Unit 5

INDIRECT COMMUNICATIONS:
WRITING NEGATIVE AND PERSUASIVE MESSAGES

Objectives

By successfully completing this unit, you will:

- learn when to write indirect messages;
- learn a model showing how to organize indirect messages;
- write indirect messages;
- edit indirect messages; and
- rewrite indirect messages.

Case Study

X-Cel Manufacturing Company has just received the results of an extensive research project completed by The Right Image, a local marketing and public relations firm. The study shows that X-Cel's profits could increase significantly if the computers were assembled in Asia, rather than at X-Cel's Mexico-based subsidiary, Aztech Assembly. X-Cel's board of directors has decided to act on The Right Image's recommendation to relocate the production operation. X-Cel's vice president of international operations must let management at Aztech know that Aztech will no longer assemble Model XL-503. The relocation of assembly will result in significant layoffs and possible loss of goodwill in the Tijuana area.

Writing Bad News and Negative Messages

Everyone has to give bad news and negative messages sometime. You may have had to tell someone that he or she did not receive an award or win an election. You may have broken up with a sweetheart or have told someone about another couple's breakup. You may have had to tell someone of the death of a friend or relative.

In business, people also have to send bad news messages. Bad news comes in many forms: rejection for employment or promotion, the denial of credit, a job resignation, a customer complaint about a product or service received from a store, a collection letter, a change in company policy, the curtailment of services—these are just a few examples.

Most people find giving bad news to be challenging or difficult for a number of reasons.

People tend to avoid conflict. Most people are uncomfortable in conflict situations. They would rather cooperate with others or find ways to maintain harmony than deal with unpleasant, negative situations. Some common misconceptions about avoiding conflict include believing that the situation will clear up by itself over time, that someone else will deal with the situation, or that the conflict really isn't important enough to worry about.

People fear losing credibility or business. Many business people believe that if they give negative feedback, they will lose the respect of their employees, peers, customers, or clients. Loss of credibility may result in loss of business. Paramount in the minds of concerned writers is the establishment and maintenance of goodwill.

People need to be liked and accepted. We all need to be liked and accepted by others. If we give negative news to someone, we may jeopardize a relationship. This underlying motivation plays a major role in whether and how we deal with negative situations.

The way in which bad news is delivered has a strong effect on how the bad news is received and on the receiver's perception of the writer's and the company's credibility. Consider the following letter from the vice president of international operations (Example 5-1). A primary reason most executives are promoted is their ability to communicate. It would be rare for a vice president to write such a letter, but let's imagine that Drew Reinhold wrote this as a first draft.

How would you feel if you were Ray Deal? Would you feel comfortable about your job? Would you want to have a plan about how to close down the plant? Would you want to have to lay off hundreds of employees? Probably not. Drew Reinhold has been too direct and negative about the situation. He could have delivered the message in a different manner, which would have been easier for Ray Deal to accept. At this point, all Ray knows is that the future looks bad. Perhaps a different approach could have been used to make the message more positive and palatable.

X-CEL MANUFACTURING COMPANY

One Washington Square, Silicon Valley, CA 90000 (408) 555-9235
Toll Free 1(800) 555-9286 FAX (408) 555-9336

May 1, 1993

Mr. Raymond Deal
Aztech Assembly
1 Ave. No. 30-80 Zona 12
Tijuana, Mexico

Dear Ray:

Well, I hate to be the bearer of bad news, but I regret that I must inform you that, effective June 15, 1993, you will be forced to close down operations at Aztech.

It seems that the members of the board of directors are so eager to make a buck that they have decided to relocate our assembly operations to Malaysia for cheaper labor.

Of course, this will require that you get rid of all of the Mexican workers there and close up shop as quickly as possible.

I'm sorry to have to inconvenience you like this, but that's the way it is. You will receive a more official announcement and instructions from the president's office later this week.

Stop by when you get back to Silicon Valley.

Sincerely,

Drew Reinhold
Vice President
International Operations

DR:jbs

Where computers are born

Example 5-1:
A Poorly Written Bad News Letter

121

This is the model Drew should have followed while writing the letter to Ray Deal.

MODEL FOR BAD NEWS
AND NEGATIVE MESSAGES

- Start with a buffer statement or paragraph.
- Present reasons for your decision.
- State your decision.
- Motivate your reader to comply with your decision.
- End on a positive, friendly note.

Note that the purpose of the message, the negative point, is not given right away, but is sandwiched between other portions of the message. This is why we call this type of message *indirect*. Let's now look at the components of the model and the rationale behind each.

Start with a buffer statement or paragraph. A buffer statement at the beginning of a negative message softens or leads up to the bad news. It typically starts off setting a positive tone for what is about to follow. It is tactful and goodwill oriented.

• **Say "Thank you."** One easy way to start a buffer statement is to say "Thank you." If a customer sends you a message complaining that the product he purchased did not perform to his satisfaction, and you are not able to make an adjustment because the warranty has expired, you would start by thanking him for writing and bringing the matter to your attention. You are showing that you are interested in feedback, regardless of whether it is positive or negative. If you need to tell a job applicant that she is no longer being considered for a position, start by thanking her for her interest in the position.

Many people have learned to spot certain bad news messages because of such buffer statements. The applicant for graduate school is waiting for a letter that starts out with "Congratulations!" When the applicant reads the first line that starts with "Thank you for applying to the Wharton M.B.A. program," it may be very clear that the decision was made to deny admission. Nevertheless, the buffer is the first attempt in the message at developing or maintaining goodwill, and goodwill receives a high priority in any business situation.

• **Compliment the other person.** Often, the person you are writing to has done a great deal of work for you or has written you a well-researched and well-supported letter regarding his or her position about something. You should acknowledge the efforts and accomplishments of others, even though you may have to deliver subsequent negative news, perhaps rejecting a proposal upon which the outstanding research is based. Your compliment would logically follow your "thank you" message.

• **Establish common ground with the other person.** Try to find a point upon which both you and your reader will agree. Or, try to show that you understand your reader's point of view. The following might be an effective buffer statement leading up to a negative message:

Thank you	Thank you for your letter of May 5, requesting funding for the computer laboratory at Marquette University.
Compliment	Your committee is to be commended on a well-researched, thoroughly documented proposal.
Common ground	Indeed, Marquette and the business community would benefit from the skills your students would gain from hands-on experience with state-of-the-art office technology.

Examples of Buffer Statements

Present the reasons for your decision.   Once you have provided a buffer statement, you will want to continue to ease into the negative news by carefully laying out the reasons for your decision. Often, if you present the reasons for your decision before you actually give someone bad news, you provide the other person with a rationale that makes it easier for that person to accept your decision. Your reasons should be presented to show your **objectivity** and your **concern for the other person.**

If you had to tell a job candidate that she was no longer being considered for a position because she lacked enough previous experience, you might focus less on her lack of experience and just let her know that you hired someone with more experience. If you needed to tell an applicant for an M.B.A. program that his grade point average and admission test scores were deficient, you would avoid telling him that he *didn't have* what it takes. You would be more tactful by explaining what you require and encouraging him to work toward achieving those scores, perhaps even giving him guidance about available resources. Consider the following messages:

	(Buffer)
Evaluative negative	Unfortunately, your grade point average was only 2.7 and your GMAT score was only 475. Obviously, you do not meet our requirements for admission, and we must reject your application.
	(Buffer)
Objective **tactful** **Reader-oriented**	Gonzaga University requires a grade point average of 3.0 and a GMAT score of 500 for a candidate to be considered for admission. Your grade point average is 2.7 and your GMAT score is 475.

Negative
blaming

The warranty on your toaster was only good for 90 days and expired on September 30. You should have submitted your claim before that date if you expected any type of refund.

Objective

All Toastmaster products carry a 90-day warranty. During the warranty period, we gladly refund the full value of any product returned by our customers. The warranty card you sent to us on November 23 shows that you purchased your toaster on July 1.

Examples of Reasons for Decisions

State your decision. Eventually, you must convey your decision to your reader. If you have been careful in presenting your reasons for your decision, you may have already made your point without explicitly stating it. In the two previous examples, if your readers are bright, you may not have to state specifically that they are not going to get what they want. They will understand your decision, based on the facts you have presented so logically and carefully. In some cases, you will want to be more emphatic; the most emphatic "no" might be "You cannot have a refund." Of course, a sensitive writer wants to try to create a softer way to state this. One common technique is, "Considering these facts, what we can do for you is. . . ."
In other words, focus less on the negative or what you cannot do and get the reader to focus more on what you can do. You can nearly always find something positive in a situation like this.

Motivate your reader to comply with your decision. Offering help in any bad news situation both encourages the other person to accept your decision and furthers your efforts to maintain goodwill.

Point out to your reader any advantages or positive outcomes of your decision. If you can provide a partial refund for the toaster, state that you are happy to provide a partial refund. Avoid stating that you cannot provide a total refund. If you are willing to provide free service instead of a refund, emphasize the free service. After presenting your reasons to the graduate school applicant about why you will not consider his application favorably at this time, you can help him get closer to his goals.

Please take your toaster to any authorized dealer, and Toastmaster will gladly have it repaired at our expense.

You may wish to enroll as an unclassified graduate student and take classes to raise your g.p.a. You may

By providing something for your readers, you give them some satisfaction, guidance, and hope, and you maintain positive relationships with them.

End on a positive, friendly note.   Once you have presented the bad news and any other necessary information, you should close your message with an attempt to encourage the other person to continue doing business with you. You may say something as simple as the following:

Please contact me if I may be of further help.

I look forward to hearing from you soon.

Please let me know soon if you would like to take advantage of this offer.

Examples of Positive/Friendly Closings

This is like putting the second piece of bread on a sandwich; you are putting the "meaty" part between two blander pieces. You should try to find something more personal and unique than trite phrases such as "Please don't hesitate to call me," or "Thank you for your time and consideration." Relate your close to your previous message.

Is it always appropriate to "sugar coat" bad news? Not necessarily. If you know that someone wants you to deliver the bad news directly, then comply. Some people do not like others to use psychology on them. Tact is good psychology in most instances, but there are exceptions to every rule. In fact, some people try to make a positive situation out of a negative one. For example, instead of regarding your resignation from a company as bad news or a negative message, could you emphasize the opportunities your new job will present? Rather than tell a customer that you no longer carry a product, could you tell the customer where to purchase the product?

Use positive/non-defensive language.   When we have something negative to say, we often naturally resort to negative language. "We regret to inform you" and "We are sorry for the inconvenience this problem may have caused you" contain negative words: *regret, sorry, inconvenience,* and *problem.* Can you think of other words that will result in a negative-sounding message? How about *no, not, never, cannot, unfortunately,* and *failed?* We have alternative ways of delivering messages that contain these words. Consider these examples:

Negative   We cannot have your car ready until Tuesday after 4 p.m.
Better   You may pick up your car on Tuesday, after 4 p.m.

Negative   Please don't hesitate to call me.
Better   Please feel free to call me any time.

You should always challenge yourself by asking if you can deliver a negative message in a more positive way. You develop a mind set that helps you quickly phrase messages in more tactful ways.

Now let's look again at Drew Reinhold's message to Ray Deal (Example 5-1). Do you see a buffer statement? Has Drew provided a rationale that would help Ray accept the bad news? Has he given Ray any motivation to carry out the task of closing down the plant? Has he written a positive, friendly close? Has he used negative words?

> Well, I hate to be the bearer of bad news, but I regret that I must inform you that, effective June 15, 1993, you will be forced to close down operations at Aztech.
>
> It seems that the members of the board of directors are so eager to make a buck that they have decided to relocate our assembly operations to Malaysia for cheaper labor.
>
> Of course, this will require that you get rid of all of the Mexican workers there and close up shop as quickly as possible.
>
> I'm sorry to have to inconvenience you like this, but thats the way it is. You will receive a more official announcement and instructions from the president's office later this week.
>
> Stop by when you get back to Silicon Valley.

Drew could have started off the letter with something as simple as "Aztech has provided X-Cel with outstanding assembly service for the past 15 years." He may have a more personal relationship with Ray, which would allow him to start off the letter with "I hope all is going well with you at Aztech." Of course, the situation will determine what must be said, but Drew needs to consider how Ray will take the news and the best way to lead into it. Ray may be ready to move back to the United States. He may wish to be transferred to Malaysia. He may be very upset about having to move. He may be excited about moving and concerned about how to terminate all of his friends and employees in Mexico. All of these possibilities (and more) must be considered before Drew writes his letter. After all, this is not a routine matter.

Drew should find out what X-Cel plans to do with the existing facilities in Tijuana. Does X-Cel plan to assemble any other products there? Will X-Cel lease or sell the plant to another company? Will the other company be able to employ all or any of the current work force? Is X-Cel prepared to provide assistance to the workers and families being affected?

Drew should also provide more information about (or at least reword) why Malaysia will be the new site for assembly. "Cheaper labor" sounds unprofessional.

Finally, Drew needs to close the letter with something positive and friendly. "Stop by when you get back to Silicon Valley" is friendly and colloquial, but this type of letter may need something more supportive. Now that we've critiqued Drew's initial letter, let's rewrite it (Example 5-2).

How would you rewrite Drew's letter?

X-CEL MANUFACTURING COMPANY

One Washington Square, Silicon Valley, CA 90000 (408) 555-9235
Toll Free 1(800) 555-9286 FAX (408) 555-9336

May 1, 1993

Mr. Raymond Deal, Production Manager
Aztech Assembly
1 Ave. No. 30-80 Zona 12
Tijuana, Mexico

Dear Ray:

Thank you for all of the excellent assembly work you and your staff have provided for
the past 15 years. With Aztech's support, we have been able to expand into the
business market, and with this expansion come many exciting opportunities.

Our latest studies indicate that we can increase profits significantly by making some
changes. Most of the changes involve our manufacturing process. The most
significant change will be to relocate our assembly operation to Malaysia, where labor
costs are lower. We've found a facility there that was used previously for computer
assembly, so we can move in immediately.

As we discussed, you are being offered two options with X-Cel. You may return to the
United States as general manager of our research and development division, or you
may move to Malaysia and continue as production manager.

Hyundai Motors has signed a lease for the existing Aztech plant. They will need about
a month to modify the CAD/CAM equipment. They have expressed a desire to employ
most of the current employees during the remodeling and to hire them as permanent
employees once they begin production.

Ray, I trust you will do everything you can to help your employees find suitable
employment with Hyundai or other employers in the area. Make this a priority item for
your personnel department. You have built such a good reputation for us with the local
community.

Please contact me as needed about the move. You will have my total cooperation in
seeing that the changes are made as smoothly as possible.

Sincerely,

Drew Reinhold

Drew Reinhold
Vice President, International Operations

DR/jbs

Where computers are born
Example 5-2
Bad News Letter

128

Note that the message suggests that Ray and Drew have already discussed this matter, and that this letter provides written documentation. Very often this is how sensitive situations are handled. Details are worked out in person; the letter follows to confirm those details.

Writing Persuasive Messages

The indirect approach is very appropriate for use in persuasive messages like sales and fund-raising letters. These are messages that need to consider the psychological strategies important in getting people to behave, think, feel in ways that you want them to behave, think, and feel. The AIDA model (Attention, Interest, Desire, and Action) is a framework that incorporates many of the psychological strategies important for persuasive messages.

MODEL FOR PERSUASIVE MESSAGES

- Get the *attention* of the receiver through the use of questions, stories or other strategies.

- Arouse *interest* by helping the reader visualize the personal benefit to be gained by what you have to offer.

- Stimulate *desire* by appealing to the personal motivations of the receiver.

- Ask for *action* by getting the receiver to do something or commit to some specific action.

Attention   The first thing that the message must do is get the receiver to look at it. There are several ways that persuasive messages can get the receiver's attention. You might ask a question, tell a story, or involve the reader in something interesting, like a short quiz or puzzle that you ask him or her to solve. Again, you must be creative to make your persuasive message stand out from all of the others that come in daily. Imagine the impact of the following question in a persuasive letter designed to solicit support for a gun control bill:

> What are your chances of becoming a victim of a crime committed
> with a handgun?

Interest and Desire   Interest and desire are treated together here because they are not mutually exclusive when you try to build them into your persuasive messages. To build interest and desire you need to mention some of the characteristics of the product or service and get the reader to visualize the *benefits* to be realized from using it. Here are some specific techniques that you can use to create interest in and desire for your idea, product, or service in the minds of your receivers.

• **Establish credibility.**   Credibility has to do with the overall believability of the message. One way of establishing credibility is to associate your message with a credible source. Source credibility is usually established by people who have certain characteristics. Normally, they have demonstrated intelligence, sound character, and a genuine interest in the goodwill of other people rather than interest only in themselves. For example, if you were

129

Normally, they have demonstrated intelligence, sound character, and a genuine interest in the goodwill of other people rather than interest only in themselves. For example, if you were trying to get people to come to an international conference on the importance of customer service, a quote from management expert Tom Peters on the value of such a conference would be most helpful in establishing credibility.

• **Use logic.** Source credibility is the believability of the person delivering the message. You can also establish *message* credibility by making the content of the message itself believable. Consider using simple logic for this, including specific facts to back up your claims. The example below shows how logic can be used in a letter designed to point out the benefits of attending a program to increase employee morale:

> Of the 347 supervisors and managers who completed the program, 318
> (92 percent) reported a noticeable increase in employee morale. All
> of the participating companies experienced an increase in productivity.

• **Appeal to emotion.** If you can get to the "feeling" level of people, you can get closer to persuading them. Any emotion that you can read—fear, love, jealousy, happiness, the desire to achieve—will bring you nearer to your objective. Using emotional appeals is very effective with consumer products. By pointing out to breadwinners that their families may really suffer if their income suddenly stops, an insurance sales representative has a pretty good chance of selling additional policies. By showing young automobile drivers pictures of accident victims, the National Safety Council may persuade some people to fasten their seat belts.

Action Developing an action close for your letter is really just a matter of trying to get the reader to do something. Here are two examples of how you might end a letter that is attempting to get participation in a training program on increasing employee morale:

> Just fill out the enclosed postage-paid card telling us that you are
> interested in our program. One of our representatives will arrange to
> meet with you to discuss the details of the training program.

> Call us at (408) 866-9000 and one of our representatives will arrange
> a time to show you how your employees may benefit from our program.

AIDA can be a very helpful tool in planning your persuasive messages. Example 5-3 shows an actual letter attempting to get money from a foundation. It so happens that this letter was successful in getting the requested contribution. How well does the letter follow the AIDA model? Does it follow the indirect approach? Are there any steps missing? How would you improve it?

BOYS CITY BOYS' CLUB OF SILICON VALLEY
1134 Technology Drive
Suite 1234
Los Gatos, CA 95120
(408) 987-5634

May 3, 1993

Ms. Ervie Jones, Executive Director
The Drew Foundation
P. O. Box 1239
San Jose, CA. 95182

Dear Ms. Jones:

After 45 years, our organization is undergoing a radical change! We are expanding and transforming our program offerings to serve a co-ed population. By the end of this spring, our Northside and Eastside units will welcome over 1,500 new members—all of them female.

These changes bring with them new challenges to an organization with a long history of service to the community. The transition to co-ed programs and facilities requires additional staffing, as well as sensitivity to issues facing women in the 1990s. We therefore anticipate adding several female staff members as well as new programs targeted to our new female group and to the co-ed population.

The Drew Foundation, with its distinguished history of promoting youth activities in Santa Clara County, is a natural partner for Boys City Boys' Clubs of Silicon Valley as it expands its traditional programs to reach previously unserved boys and girls. On behalf of the more than 3,000 low-income and at-risk boys and girls served by our organization, I would like to request $35,000 from The Drew Foundation. These funds would be utilized in receiving over 1,500 girls into an organization that has been traditionally limited to boys.

We would enjoy receiving an invitation to submit a full proposal and the opportunity to work with you to serve young people in our community. Thank you for considering our request, and we are looking forward to hearing from you.

Sincerely,

Don Green, Executive Director

Example 5-3
Asking for Funds

131

Exercises:

The following exercises have been included to help you prepare for writing bad news and indirect messages. As you complete each one, ask yourself, "What am I trying to do here?" Each section builds on the previous section, so that by the end of the exercises you will have written six complete bad news messages.

Start with a Buffer Statement

Write a buffer statement for each of the following situations.

1. Tell a job applicant that she is no longer being considered for employment with your company.

2. Turn down an applicant for a credit card with your company.

3. Tell a business associate that you will not be able to attend a meeting he has organized.

4. Tell a representative of an organization that you will not be able to speak at a meeting.

5. Tell a customer that you will not refund money on a product he used improperly.

6. Tell an advertiser that you do not wish to advertise in a publication.

Provide Reasons for Your Decision

For each of the following situations, provide an organized rationale for your decision. Try to be objective, reader-oriented, and tactful. These situations are extensions of the previous exercise on buffer statements.

1. The candidate you are turning down for employment earned her B.S. degree in finance and has two years' experience as a bank teller while working her way through school. You found another, more suitable candidate with a four-year degree in business administration with over two years' hands-on experience with management information systems. The finance major expressed a strong interest in your company, showing that she had done extensive research into the company's history and plans for future development. Your company has a financial management training program that might be more appropriate for this candidate.

2. The applicant for a credit card has been with his current employer for one month. His annual salary is $25,000. He has one other credit card. Your company requires that credit applicants have worked at their current job at least six months, have an annual income of $18,000, and have previous credit history. You believe that this applicant will be a good credit risk.

3. A business associate at another company has invited you and several members of your company to attend a seminar on advances in the telecommunications field. You are interested in the subject, but your company has scheduled its annual picnic for that day, July 16. All of those invited are senior managers. A new employee has volunteered to attend the seminar to take notes for your management team. You would like to send her.

4. The program chairman of the local chapter of the Institute of Internal Auditors has requested that you speak at the chapter's monthly meeting on October 15. The members want to learn more about how to make effective oral presentations to managers. You have spoken at many professional meetings over the years, and have gained an excellent reputation. However, you and your family have a vacation planned during that time. You are aware that the local Toastmasters organization will send representatives to speak at such meetings.

5. You received a letter from a customer who lives halfway across the country that his new power saw is not working properly after only six months. After further investigation, your customer service department has found that he purchased a light-duty saw, generally good for cutting boards and plywood. The customer has been using the saw to cut large fence posts and tree limbs. You have several other heavy-duty saws designed for thicker pieces of wood. Very clear instructions and usage limitations are provided with each saw.

6. Your public relations company representative has encouraged you to place an advertisement in a publication that contains advertisements for other products that you believe would hurt the image of your company. In fact, you are insulted to have even been asked to consider such a move, but your representative has been a risk taker all along.

State Your Decision

For each of the preceding situations (buffer statement exercises and rationale exercises), write out your decision the way you would in a letter. Decide whether you need to state your negative decision explicitly, whether you have already implied your decision in your reasons section, and whether you can actually turn this into a positive message.

1.

2.

3.

4.

5.

6.

Motivate Your Reader to Comply with Your Decision

1. Encourage the job applicant to apply for your financial management training program.

2. Encourage the credit card applicant to reapply after he has worked for his current employer for six months.

3. Emphasize that you are sending someone to the seminar who is eager to learn what the other company is offering.

4. Encourage the program chairman to contact the local chapter of Toastmasters, or offer to contact them for him.

5. Encourage the customer to have his saw serviced at an authorized dealership or to purchase one of your saws that is intended for heavy-duty use.

6. Encourage your public relations representative to find a more appropriate outlet for your advertising dollars.

End on a Positive, Friendly Note

For each of the situations above, provide a positive, friendly close that will maintain goodwill and encourage the other person to continue doing business with your company.

1.

2.

3.

4.

5.

6.

Write, Edit, Rewrite

Your company has provided financial support for outstanding students at a local university for the past five years. You have donated money for scholarships and other awards. This year, your budget committee decided to discontinue this support. The members believe that other companies should have a turn. They have also found the return on investment to be low. None of the recipients of scholarships has accepted a position with your company; in fact, most have left the area. You have received a letter from the university requesting that you donate money again this year.

1. In the space below, write a first draft to Dr. Jesse Lara at the school of business of a university in your area. Follow the model presented earlier: Start with a buffer statement; organize your reasons for your decision; motivate your reader to accept your decision; end on a positive, friendly note. Remember, you want to maintain good relations with the university; you just don't want to donate money this year.

2. Review and edit the first draft of your letter. Highlight any areas that need improvement. Have you provided a smooth buffer? Have you organized your reasons in such a way that Dr. Lara will understand and accept your decision? Have you provided any guidance or alternative sources for Dr. Lara? Have you ended on a positive, friendly note? Have you eliminated all of the negative language and flag words? Write notes in the margins; use proofreader's marks, etc.

3. Rewrite your message, based on your editing efforts. Does the message sound better? Have you followed the model presented in this unit? Have you eliminated potential sources of embarrassment? Edit and rewrite your message again, if necessary.

Homework Problems

Manufacturing Company

Manufacturing Company to Assembly Company You are concerned because your legal adviser has called to your attention the fact that your subsidiary assembly company in Mexico employs very few Mexican nationals in management ranks. In fact, only two Mexican employees fill first-line supervisor positions, and there are none above this level. Your legal counsel fears that a lawsuit may be filed by the Mexican government to force hiring more locals into management positions. Write a letter to your counterpart in the assembly company, indicating your concern and proposing that they begin to make plans to change this situation. You are aware of possible negative reactions such a letter will generate from that company's management.

Manufacturing Company to Supply Company Your company has been approached by a Japanese supply company who is asking your management to contract with them to be the exclusive supplier of parts for the XL503. They claim that their parts pass quality-control standards that are higher than any other in the world. They guarantee on-time deliveries, quality parts, excellent service, and the lowest prices in the marketplace. Your management has decided to sign the contract. Of course, this means that you will have to sever your relationship and agreements with your current suppliers. Write to your counterpart in the supply company.

Manufacturing Company to Software Company The software company just finished designing software for the XL503. This new program was designed to be the most powerful financial spreadsheet package yet. It was advertised to be available next month. However, the modifications you needed to make to the XL503 have been delayed. In fact, you have run into a legal problem in getting parts from the supplier. Apparently, a competitor holds the patent on the printed circuit board you need to add to the computer, and that company will not allow you to use the board in your machine. Now, you have to design and manufacture your own board, and this will delay the project at least two weeks. You are afraid you will lose retail business, and you are certain that the software company will be upset. You don't want software to sever its relationship with your company and sign a contract with your competitor. Write to your counterpart in the software company, telling of the delay and encouraging patience until you can have the part ready for production.

Manufacturing Company to Retail Company You have discovered that the retail store is selling a Taiwanese-made clone of your XL503 computer. You filed a criminal complaint in Taiwan, charging that a group of Taiwanese businessmen illegally cloned your popular XL503 and have infringed on your trademarks and advertisements. Your investigators also found pirated software being sold along with the computers. While you believe that the retailers thought that they were receiving authentic merchandise from authorized representatives, you must tell them to remove all cloned merchandise from their shelves. This may cost the retailers, since they have already purchased the clones from the Taiwanese. Write to your counterpart in the retail company, requesting that the merchandise be removed from the store.

Manufacturing Company to Public Relations Company Your company typically spends millions of dollars each year for advertising. You have used glossy image brochures, full-page magazine and newspaper ads, and radio and television blitzes to encourage further patronage and to announce employment opportunities. Your top officers have slashed your advertising budget from $30 million to $20 million for the next year. They want to look into the effectiveness of current advertising methods and consider alternative ways to reach the public.

Write to your counterpart in the public relations company, explaining that you will not be placing as many ads during the next fiscal year.

Assembly Company

Assembly Company to Manufacturing Company Juan Garcia is one of two first-line supervisors in the plant. Juan has been a good supervisor, but over the past year he has had many problems. Juan lost his wife in an automobile accident and since has had troubles with his own life. He continually misses work and rarely arrives at work on time. He has missed an average of one day a week over the last six months. He has been talked to and warned many times, but he has not improved his performance. On a number of occasions he has shown up for work with liquor on his breath. You have decided to terminate Juan. Write a letter to Juan to let him know your decision. Send a copy to your counterpart in the manufacturing company.

Assembly Company to Supply Company A recent order you received from the supply company contained 2,000 printed circuit boards. After you had begun applying the circuitry, one of your technicians discovered that the boards are 1/32" too large to fit into their designated space. You need the boards for this order, but cannot take the time to trim them to fit. You must return them to the supply company and get credit or, preferably, a replacement. Write to your counterpart in the supply company, telling of the order you received and asking for an adjustment.

Assembly Company to Software Company You have received several visits and telephone calls from a local university telling you that the software used by local Mexican students contains incorrect translations for Mexico. Further investigation revealed that much of the information seemed to be written by someone who had studied Spanish in the United States, and that the idioms and word usage reflected more how the language is spoken in Spain than in Mexico. You realize that it would be culturally appropriate to modify the software to meet the needs of the market. Write to your counterpart in the software company, telling of this need for correction.

Assembly Company to Retail Company You rely on U.S. trucking firms to transport finished computers to retail distributors. The trucking industry has just announced a 4 percent increase in freight rates; this is the second time rates have been raised in six months. Consequently, you must increase the price of the computers you assemble. The retail stores will pay more for the computers they sell to their customers, but, of course, they will pass this extra cost on in the form of higher retail prices. Write a letter to your counterpart in the retail company, telling of the increased cost of your computers.

Assembly Company to Public Relations Company Your management has noticed recently that your company's image in the community seems to be changing. The managers believe that the public relations campaign and some of the advertising are not on target. In fact, you believe that some of your messages might even be insulting and condescending to the Mexican community. In a recent meeting, one of your colleagues accused the public relations company of negligence for not considering the cultural issues involved in effective advertising and community relations. You have been asked to relay this information to your counterpart in the public relations company.

Supply Company

Supply Company to Manufacturing Company You supply parts to computer manufacturers and other companies using computer assisted manufacturing (CAM) equipment. Recently, the machine tool industry has experienced quite a slump, which is expected to continue for some time. Orders are down; profits have declined. This has had an enormous impact on the automobile and truck industry and on defense contractors, all major machine users. Many of the lathes and milling machines are equipped with electronic controls. You have always counted on large orders from companies in this industry, but now business is bad. Consequently, you will be forced to raise your prices to computer manufacturers. The prices of all of your components and other parts will be increased by 8 percent. Write to your counterpart in the manufacturing company, telling of the price increase.

Supply Company to Assembly Company You learned today that you recently shipped several thousand faulty computer boards to various customers. The boards were designed incorrectly and cause the entire system to crash. If your estimates are correct, the boards will have already been installed in many of your customers' computers. You need to recall all of the boards with serial numbers starting with DT614. This means that companies will have to disassemble finished computers and work in process, as well as return all boards still in the raw materials stage. Write to your counterpart in the assembly company to recall these boards.

Supply Company to Software Company A couple of years ago, the software company impressed upon your company the importance of having the right image projected by their product, specifically in its packaging. One objective was to have customized labels for the diskettes. They made it clear to your company that they would "take their business elsewhere" if you couldn't provide the customized labels. You arranged with a local printer to have these printed at a reasonable rate. Yesterday, the printer called you to tell you that he was going out of business and that he had no back stock of the labels. You have an order from the software company for 500,000 diskettes with labels. You believe that you can find another printer, but you realize that this will mean a delay of about three weeks. Write to your counterpart in the software company.

Supply Company to Retail Company Your company is planning to discontinue making a plastic reenforcing shield that protects the wiring harness used in the XL503. The costs of plastic and manufacturing make it no longer profitable to manufacture the part. Other companies manufacture the part at a higher price. Write to your counterpart in the retail company. Let this person know your decision and that you plan to phase out the manufacturing of the part within three months.

Supply Company to Public Relations Company Your public relations company recently proposed to "give your company a face lift" to make it appear more "high- tech." They conducted a study of your customers and competitors and found that your company is considered the "dinosaur" of the industry. The building is old; it needs painting both inside and outside. Your delivery trucks look more like what construction companies use than the mini-vans used by the other more streamlined companies. Your staff are wearing overalls and aprons, much as warehouse workers wore years ago. Your management believes that this is the image they want. They like the look of experience and stability—an old-fashioned, work- hard ethic. Write to your counterpart in the public relations company to reject the offer to renovate your company.

Software Company

Software Company to Manufacturing Company You learned recently that the manufacturing company has an assembly plant in Johannesburg, South Africa. Your company took a stand against apartheid and agreed to boycott any companies doing business or having investments in South Africa. Your company is a racially balanced, equal opportunity employer, and your officers believe that adhering to such a policy is the ethical thing to do. Write to your counterpart in the manufacturing company, explaining your company's policy and asking for an explanation of what the manufacturing company plans to do about its operations in South Africa.

Software Company to Assembly Company Your counterpart in the assembly company has written to you to request that your company develop software programs in Spanish for the Mexican market. Your company does not have staff who are bilingual in Spanish, nor is it in your company's plans to even attempt such a project through outside consultants. You also know that several companies already have cornered the market, so why should you even try to be "just one more software package"? Write to your counterpart in the assembly company to turn down the request.

Software Company to Supply Company You are concerned about the quality of the mother boards that you receive from your supplier to test your software. The last shipment of 15 boards had seven faulty boards. This is not the first time this has happened; the previous shipment of 10 boards had three faulty boards. The faulty boards are causing your organization delays in testing and product development. You want the supply company to credit your account for the faulty boards, and you want a guarantee that the quality problem will be corrected soon, or you will begin to look for another supplier. Write to your counterpart in the supply company, letting that person know about the latest shipment.

Software Company to Retail Company Your company has sent out "shoppers" into the retail stores to see how store clerks promote your software. The shoppers found that many of the clerks not only did not know much about how to use the software, but they made negative comments about its usefulness as well. Your company has always had a policy of providing training for retail personnel so that they would be able to promote the software. You are concerned that this behavior occurs in the stores. Write to your counterpart in the retail company, telling about your shoppers' observations.

Software Company to Public Relations Company Your marketing department has advised management that it is time to switch to a new advertising and public relations company. Your current public relations company does not really understand the software market as well as you would like, and you believe that you can get better service through The Right Image, one of Silicon Valley's leading public relations companies. Write to your counterpart in the public relations company, telling of your management's decision to change companies.

Retail Company

Retail Company to Manufacturing Company One of your representatives recently visited the manufacturing company. Upon her return she was angry and filed a complaint with her boss. She stated that while she was touring the assembly line, she noticed posters and calendars of naked women decorating the walls. She was stared at, whistled at, and even patted by one of the male workers. When she asked one of the female secretaries if this went on very often, the secretary replied, "Yes, but we've gotten used to it." Appalled, she returned

145

to your store and reported the incident. You have been asked to write to your counterpart to get a formal apology from the company. You have also been asked to inquire about what the company plans to do about sexual harassment in the workplace. The woman involved in the incident is threatening to file a sexual harassment lawsuit against the company.

Retail Company to Assembly Company The last shipment of connector cables for your machines had been assembled with the wrong "male" ends. It is impossible to insert the plug into the outlet on the back of the XL503. You received 50 computers with faulty cables, plus an additional 15 cables for your service center. Write to your counterpart in the assembly company, telling of the incorrect cables.

Retail Company to Supply Company The sales representative from your supplier is a hard-sell type. He often puts pressure on your store managers to order more than they need. Just before the supply company phased out a part, the sales representative managed to "unload" 500 soon-to-be-obsolete printed circuit boards at a number of your stores. You believe that this was unethical and want the supply company to take back the merchandise and credit your account. You also want assurance that this type of practice will never happen again. Write to your counterpart in the supply company.

Retail Company to Software Company The software company has recently made a takeover bid to your company. They offered $693.9 million two months ago, but you turned down their offer. They are currently offering you $1.69 billion in common stock, and the company's stock is doing well on the New York Stock Exchange. Your company officers are still not ready to be taken over; they believe that they can still get a better deal. They would like to see some real estate and buildings as part of the negotiation. Write a letter to your counterpart in the software company, refusing the current bid.

Retail Company to Public Relations Company You are unhappy with Sarah Williams, manager of your advertising account from the marketing and public relations company. Sarah is new to your account and seems to have definite ideas about what she thinks needs to be done. She handles magazine advertisements, and tells you that your company needs a fresh approach. You believe that the previous advertising approach, with its emphasis on complete sales and service, has worked well. Why change when things are going so well? Write to your counterpart in the public relations company. Let this person know that you do not want Sarah Williams to handle your account any longer. You do not like her ideas or her personality. You think that she is too aggressive and is not interested in your ideas.

Public Relations Company

Public Relations Company to Manufacturing Company Your company has just participated in a major study for the U.S. government. The study investigated companies to determine whether any were in violation of child labor law regulations. Numerous companies across the nation were found operating outside of the law. While none of your clients was found in violation through the study, your computer manufacturing account is known to stretch some of the laws to meet its needs. It employs some high school teenagers who operate forklifts and other motorized vehicles prohibited by law. Some of these students work after school, but are often scheduled to work into the later evening hours. The law clearly states that children should not work late. The officials at the local school district complain that students who work late often fall asleep in class. Write to your counterpart, reporting the findings of the study and your recommendations.

146

Public Relations Company to Assembly Company   Your assembly company account asked you to develop new advertisements designed to describe their interest in implementing quality circles and participative decision-making techniques in their organization.   You consulted with one of your associates who is well acquainted with the various cultures within Mexico, and he was skeptical about whether this focus would attract members of the Mexican community. He stated that his understanding of Mexican employees is that most are so used to taking orders from the *patron* (boss) that it would be extremely difficult for them to feel comfortable treating the boss as an equal or offering candid input. After careful consideration, you have decided that perhaps the assembly company should not place such an advertisement. Write to your counterpart in the assembly company to tell this news.

Public Relations Company to Supply Company   You have just completed a market study for your supply company account. You were asked to find out the attitudes and perceptions that customers and potential customers have about the supply company. You found that many people said that they stopped purchasing from the supply company because the order clerks and delivery personnel were rude to customers. Respondents also said that many of the parts put together by technicians at the company had to be returned because of faulty soldering. Turn-around time on orders seemed a bit too long to many customers, who believe that the company needs to computerize its sales and inventory procedures. Most people surveyed agreed that the company needs to update its image, even to go so far as to paint the outside of the building and to buy some new equipment, trucks, and furniture. Write a letter to your counterpart in the supply company, giving your findings and recommendations.

Public Relations Company to Software Company   You have just completed a marketing research study for the software company. You were commissioned by the company to explore the market potential for a new product, *Edutech*, a software package for the education market. The software combines word processing and spreadsheet capabilities in one package. Your research suggests that there are already more competitive products on the market and your survey data suggest the product is not unique enough to carve out a market niche. Write a letter to your counterpart in the software company and tell that person that the software company should not attempt to market the product. Prepare your case carefully, because the software company has spent over two years and considerable funds developing this product.

Public Relations Company to Retail Company   You have just completed a thorough study for your retail stores account. Store management asked you to conduct a feasibility study to see if products created by the store's service technicians had a chance to succeed on the market. You have surveyed hundreds of potential customers and tested the products to determine their ability to withstand day-to-day wear and tear. You have found that there is nothing unique about the computer tables and chairs they want to manufacture and sell. The disk file cabinets have faulty hinges that break easily. Potential customers do not like the logo on the computer carrying case. Write a letter to your counterpart in the retail store, reporting your findings and recommendations.

Unit 6

BUSINESS PROPOSALS:
WRITING AND PRESENTING MORE DETAILED MESSAGES

Objectives

By successfully completing this unit, you will:

- define your proposal objective specifically and concisely;
- learn a model showing how to organize proposals;
- prepare professional visual aids;
- write a business proposal; and
- present your proposal in a business setting.

Case Study

Amerimex Assembly spends an average of $2.7 million annually in inventory holding costs; this includes rent, maintenance and repair the warehouses, salaries for warehouse employees and supervisors, equipment, supplies, inventory taxes, and more. Durango Electronics Supply Company (DESC) provides just-in-time (JIT) delivery to manufacturing and assembly companies. JIT delivery requires forecasts of assembly needs so that only the amount of inventory needed per day/week/project is delivered. If deliveries are on time, companies only need a small amount of space for their inventories. This system allows companies to reduce inventory holding costs. Ben Harrosh, sales manager at DESC, has been asked to coordinate a project team assigned to write a proposal to Amerimex. DESC would like Amerimex to adopt this JIT program.

Planning Business Proposals

Occasionally, you will be asked to write business proposals. Proposals persuade others to accept something you offer them. Business proposals also contain some element of risk. Rarely is something given for nothing. The risk may involve money, time, commitment, or a variety of other concerns and resources.

Proposals may be written to people both inside and outside the company. Internal proposals may recommend changes or suggest improvements within the company, and should

149

follow a memorandum format. External proposals range from sales proposals to suggestions to cooperate on sponsorship of an event to takeovers and mergers; while the content may be similar to an internal proposal, the format might be more formal.

One common model for organizing business proposals is to show a need for what you are proposing and then show your reader how what you offer fills that need.

MODEL FOR
BUSINESS PROPOSALS

- Show a need for what you are proposing.
- Show the effects of not accepting your proposal.
- Present a variety of possible solutions to the problem.
- State your proposal as being the best solution.
- Support your proposal by showing its advantages.
- Specify how your proposal will be implemented.
- Itemize the cost of your proposal.
- Request some type of action from your reader.

Show a need for what you are proposing. In the beginning of your proposal, you should provide a rationale for what you are proposing; that is, you present a problem that needs solving. If you are about to propose a fund-raiser, show the need for more funds. If you are proposing a cost-saving program, show that the costs are high. In our earlier case, pointing out that $2.7 million is being spent unnecessarily on inventory holding costs would provide a rationale.

Show the effects of not accepting your proposal. Next, you might project what could happen if the situation you have identified is left unattended. Show what will happen if you run out of funds and do not replace or increase them through a fund-raiser. Point out all of the money that will be wasted and the profits that will be lost if inventory remains at its current levels.

Present a variety of possible solutions to the problem. Many proposals consider alternative solutions to the problem before presenting the proposed solution. You should consider this as further support for your solution. If you can discredit all of the conceivable and probable alternatives that your reader might ask about before you present your solution, you should cause the reader to focus more on what you present.

State your proposal as being the best solution. Once you have presented the alternative solutions and have indicated some of their limitations, you have set the stage to state your proposal.

Support your proposal by showing its advantages. Next, you want to show clearly the advantages of your proposal. You might need to refer to the alternative solutions for comparison.

Specify how your proposal will be implemented. Once you have stated your proposal and its advantages, you need to assure others that it can be implemented. If you can specify

150

where, when, and how what you propose will take place, tell who will do it, and tell who will be affected by it, you fill in the details that need to be given.

Itemize the cost of your proposal. The "bottom line" to most business people is cost. "What will this cost?" is the frequent reply. You should present an open, itemized cost statement for your proposal.

Request some type of action from your reader. After you present your proposal, you should ask your reader for some commitment; whether you simply want your reader to read the proposal and contact you, or whether you want the reader to sign a contract or give you money, ask your reader to commit to some action.

Defining Your Problem

When you are about to prepare a proposal, ask yourself, "What am I trying to do?" Then define what you are trying to do in one sentence. For example, in the above scenario, Durango Electronics Supply Company's problem is to persuade the management of Amerimex to adopt Durango's just-in-time delivery system. This is a simple statement that keeps the problem simple. Everything, then, should focus on persuading Amerimex's management to decide to adopt the system.

Anticipating Your Reader's Questions

You should always try to anticipate the questions that your reader will have about your proposal. This helps you plan the content of your document. Here are some questions that are frequently asked by management regarding business proposals.

How will this project benefit our organization? People want to know how a project is going to affect them. In an organization, some key concerns are how the project will increase productivity, improve quality and efficiency, reduce people problems (turnover, absenteeism, low morale, job dissatisfaction, etc.), and solve particular organizational problems.

How much will the project cost? Crucial to the development of any proposal is a well-thought-out budget. The "bottom line" to most business people is cost. What will the entire proposal cost (consultant, materials, etc.)? What will it cost in terms of the time lost by people needed to set it up, participate, etc.?

Will the project interfere with our production schedule? Projects always involve taking people away from their jobs. When will the project begin and end? If you collect survey data, you require people to spend time answering questions. If you make organizational changes, they interrupt work time. Try to have an idea of how much "down time" your project will require; assure others that it will be minimal and worth the time.

How will you measure to see if the project has been effective? Often people complete a project, but they do not measure to see if it has been effective. After a training program has been delivered, the consultant needs to be clear on whether any results can be measured. When and how often after the project will measurement occur?

What people in the organization will be involved in this project? You need to identify which people will be involved in your proposed project. Who will it affect? Who do you need to help you coordinate it? Who is the target population of your project?

151

Why are you proposing this when we already know the results? Some skeptics will tell you they already know the outcome of your proposed project: If it is a research project, "we already know"; if it is a training session, "you can't change people"; it'll never work."

What do you know about how our organization really functions? Outsiders are often treated as not having any idea about how "our company" works. Consultants and researchers are considered out of touch with the real world.

What if the outcome of this project is negative? One thing about proposals is that you shouldn't guarantee results unless you are prepared to be held accountable. Know what you are willing to guarantee; when you cannot guarantee your results, be open and say so.

How will you get support for this from the people affected? If you are involving people other than those you are proposing to, let them know what groundwork you have already done in getting others to cooperate. You should have all of this done ahead of time.

Will you work closely with our personnel? How closely will you work with the personnel of the company? Clarify which people are involved. Try to involve credible people so that you get further support from others. Some skeptics are afraid that the process and results will be known by the wrong people.

Writing Your Proposal

Proposals may vary in size from a page to several volumes, depending upon their nature, how complicated they are, and how much additional documentation needs to be appended. For example, you may be asked to submit a one-page proposal to request money for a company picnic, but an independent contractor might submit a 200-page report to NASA when bidding on a contract for the space program. Most of the time, you should strive for conciseness to increase the likelihood of your proposal being read.

Organizing and Outlining Your Proposal

Once you have determined the content of your proposal and have an idea of how you want to organize it, you should develop an outline—for several reasons:

To organize the entire structure of your proposal This helps you get an idea of the order of your proposal. You can gain a feel for how you can best get your point across to your reader.

To group information that is naturally related This ensures that you talk about each separate topic as an individual unit without having to jump around, appearing unorganized.

To emphasize main ideas By placing your main ideas strategically throughout your outline and proposal, you give the desired amount of attention or emphasis to them. You should give equal emphasis to equally important points. Placement and parallel structure are techniques that can be used for emphasis.

To visualize how your proposal will be read by your receiver Once you have your outline in front of you, you can evaluate the psychological effect it will have on your readers. If you can put yourself in their place, you can try to guess how they might react to each element of the proposal. As an organizational tool, the outline will help you restructure the proposal if you believe it is necessary to do so.

To ensure that you include everything you intended   A good outline gives you a guide to see whether your proposal will be complete. Does your outline contain all of the points you want to include? Have you omitted anything?

To determine if you have included enough supporting material   You should try to provide a rationale for everything in your proposal. Outlining helps you determine if you have enough information for each point. You can also see the order in which you wish to place your supporting material (weakest argument to strongest argument, cause-effect, etc.).

To maximize the effectiveness of your outline, you should follow some simple guides that are basic to good organization.

OUTLINING GUIDES

- Each unit in the outline should contain only one item or statement.
- Items must be properly subordinated.
- Outlines should be prepared with proper indentation.
- You should use a definite set of outlining symbols.

Each unit in the outline should contain only one item or statement. Keep individual topics separate so that you can easily see where they belong. This is where index cards help. If you decide to merge topics, you can easily clip two or more cards together. Parallelism is important here. Use all sentences or all fragments. If you are clever, you can use your outline topics as captions throughout your proposal.

Items must be properly subordinated. Place related topics together. You need to decide which points support other points. Then, you need to decide which are the main points and which are the subordinated points.

Outlines should be prepared with proper indentation. You will easily see how topics are related and subordinated if you indent them under each topic.

You should use a definite set of outlining symbols. Roman numerals and Arabic numerals and letters should be used as symbols.

Here is a sample outline.

Adopting a JIT Inventory System at Amerimex:
A Proposal from Durango Electronics Supply Company

Outline

I. The need for a JIT program
    A.   High Inventory Holding Costs
    B.   Increasing Rate of Inventory Holding Costs
       1.   Rising 3 percent per year
       2.   Increasing inventory volume
    C.   Alternatives to Dealing with Problem
II.   The JIT Program

```
      A.   Description of Program
      B.   Benefits of Program
      C.   Implementation of Program
      D.   Costs of Program
III.   Action for Amerimex.
      A.   Summary of Problem
      B.   Summary of JIT Program
      C.   Steps Amerimex May Take

                  Example 6-1
                Proposal Outline
```

Remember, use your outline as a tool to help you organize your proposal. Change it as necessary. Move things around. Decide how things fit together. If you make organizational decisions as you write your proposal, the outline you started with should differ from the outline of your proposal once it is finished.

Using Graphs, Charts and Other Visuals

Use visuals to strengthen and clarify your proposal. When you want to clarify or strengthen your verbal message, you may wish to use visuals. Visuals include charts, graphs, tables, pictures, and other illustrations. Visuals often add credibility to your document. Some readers are impressed by visuals, and they tend to remember the information longer if it is supported by the graphic aid. Trying to explain or interpret data in paragraph form may cause confusion and boredom. Be sure that your visual has an appropriate purpose in your report or proposal; inappropriate visuals may signal the reader that you didn't really have that much to say, so you drew a picture.

Avoid using visual aids to distort data or deceive readers; make them accurate and clear. If you cannot make your visual clear and understandable, do not include it. It should clarify your report. If it has to be studied carefully, it slows down the smooth reading of your report. If it distorts the truth or deceives the reader, you should examine both the visual and your conscience.

Explain your visual aid. Don't make your visual do *all* the work. It should complement your accompanying message.

Placement of Visuals

Introduce each visual aid. Tell your reader what your visual is designed to illustrate.

Place your visual aid as near your explanation as possible, preferably immediately following it. Visuals should not interfere with the report; they should fit smoothly into its flow. Small visuals, less than one page in size, can fit neatly into the text and may be referred to easily. Large or multi-page visuals that separate pages of the text should be placed where they can be referred to, but where they do not interfere with the reading of the text. Typically, you may put these larger, more complex visuals at the end of the report, giving your reader directions in the text on where to find them. Notice how many textbooks have appendixes at the end; the authors want to include the information, but they believe it is more appropriate to attach it at the end, enhancing the smooth flow of the text.

Center your visual on the page; surround it with an appropriate amount of white space, for emphasis. *Where* you place your visual on the page is also important. It should *look* as if it belongs there. Avoid crowding visuals too close to the text. Keep your visual within the left and right margins of the text. Based on your intent and your knowledge of your reader(s), you have to judge the importance you want to give to visuals. Part of the emphasis will come from placement.

Enclose your visual in a box, if possible, for aesthetics. Another way to make your visual more attractive and to give it the emphasis it deserves is to give it a "finishing touch" by enclosing it in a box.

Clarity of Visuals

Simplify visual aids if possible; keep them brief. Because the purpose of visual aids is to clarify something that might be more difficult to understand in text form, you should make every effort to keep your illustration simple and brief. This will require your imagination, logic, and creativity.

Number each visual aid in a proposal or report. Numbering each illustration (Chart 1, Table 3, Graph 2, etc.) provides a sense of order for your paper. It is easier to refer to "Graph 2" than to refer to "the graph that shows the supplies industries' leaders in the just-in-time inventory system."

Title each visual aid so that it is clear what it illustrates. Selecting an appropriate title for an illustration requires thought. Try to keep the titles brief, but use as many words as necessary to reflect accurately what the visual shows. *Gross National Product* might not be as clear as *Changes in United States Gross National Product: 1974-1994*.

Label each part of the visual aid. Label each segment of a pie graph, each bar of a bar chart, each line of a line graph, each axis on a line graph, etc. If you have prepared your visual accurately, your reader will know what each part means.

Professionalism of Visuals

Use black or blue ink to match your type. Avoid using pencil or crayons for visuals. You can easily obtain *drawing* pencils, if you need them for shading. Computer graphics and color plotters make professional visuals. If you do not have access to these tools, at least try to make your visuals appear as if they belong in your text.

Type your labels. Avoid writing in the labels by hand. With computers graphics, press-on letters, art supplies, etc., you can produce quality labels for your visuals. See if your company has a graphic arts department where you can get assistance with visuals.

Give credit for borrowed visuals. If you reproduce a visual from another source, include a note within the visual, telling your reader where you found the original. You can make it as simple as *Source:* Arminio Fraga, *German Reparations and Brazilian Debt: A Comparative Study*, Princeton Essays in International Finance, no. 163 (Princeton, N.J., 1986).

Types of Visuals

Probably the most common types of visual aids are tables, pie graphs, line graphs, and bar graphs. You can be creative by turning more representative pictures into graphs. For example, the results of a "yes-no" poll can be represented by a "thumbs up" picture with the percentage of "yes" responses within the hand; the "thumbs down" can show the negative vote. If you wanted to show what percentage of the U. S. population owned General Motors, American Motors, Ford, and imported cars, you could shade sections of a map of the United States to represent the appropriate percentages of car owners. Let's look at the more traditional visuals.

Tables

Tables are typically used to present quantitative information in reports and proposals. Tables should be:

- Numbered.
- Titled.
- Labeled.
- Neat.
- Professional.

Read this paragraph quickly:

After using just-in-time delivery for one year, six of our customers experienced a significant decrease in inventory holding costs. Vision Tech spent $247,579 the year before JIT and only $102,653 after JIT; this was a savings of $144,926 or a decrease of 58.54 percent. CET spent $357,975 before JIT and $237,965 after; the savings was $120,010 or 33.52 percent. Advantech spent $456,879 before JIT and $247,986 after; they saved $208,893 or 45.72 percent. APEX spent $365,878 before JIT and only $198,765 after; they saved $167,113 or 45.67 percent. Supply Ltd. spent $256,650 before JIT and $150,999 after; they saved $105,651 or 41.17 percent. IDEAS spent $402,800 before JIT and $298,980 after; they saved $103,820 or 25.77 percent.

See how much easier it is to understand when it is presented in an easy-to-scan table (Table 1).

Table 1
Reduction in Inventory Holding Costs
after First Year of Just-in-Time

Company	Before JIT	After JIT	$ Decrease	% Decrease
Vision Tech	$247,579	$102,653	$144,926	58.54
CET	$357,975	$237,965	$120,010	33.52
Advantech	$456,879	$247,986	$208,893	45.72
APEX	$365,878	$198,765	$167,113	45.67
Supply Ltd.	$256,650	$150,999	$105,651	41.17
IDEAS	$402,800	$298,980	$103,820	25.77

Example 6-2
Table

Pie Graphs

Use a pie or circle graph to indicate percentages of a whole unit. Think of it as a silver dollar with so many (per)cents going to various expenses. Besides having a number (i.e., Graph 1) and a title, a pie graph should be constructed following some basic guidelines.

- **Start at the 12 o'clock position.**
- **Start with the largest percentage.**
- **Move clockwise, decreasing in percentage.**
- **Label all sections clearly.**
- **Check to see it adds up to 100 percent.**

It is easier to visualize the breakdown of expenses as percentages if they are presented in a pie graph. Consider the difference between the following paragraph and Graph 1.

Warehouse operating expenses for Amerimex can be broken down as follows: Salaries—$198,000 (55.93%); Rent—$96,000 (27.12%); Supplies—$47,000 (13.28%); and Utilities—$13,000 (3.67%).

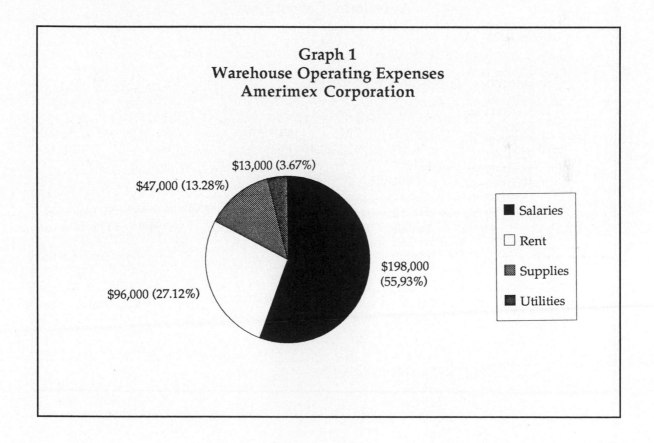

Example 6-3
Pie Graph

157

Line Graphs

Use line graphs to show trends over a period of time. Besides giving it a number and a title, you should construct a line graph following these basic guidelines:

- **Use a zero base.**
- **Use equal intervals on each axis.**
- **Label all parts clearly.**
- **Connect the points with a continuous line.**

To state that "inventory holding costs have been rising steadily since 1987" may have a slight impact on your reader. To be more specific and say that "inventory holding costs were slightly below $150,000 in 1987 and have risen to almost $450,000 in 1993" should have a stronger impact. To illustrate this steady increase over the 10-year period through a line graph normally does a better job and gives the reader more to study. Of course, providing back-up data for each year is even more helpful.

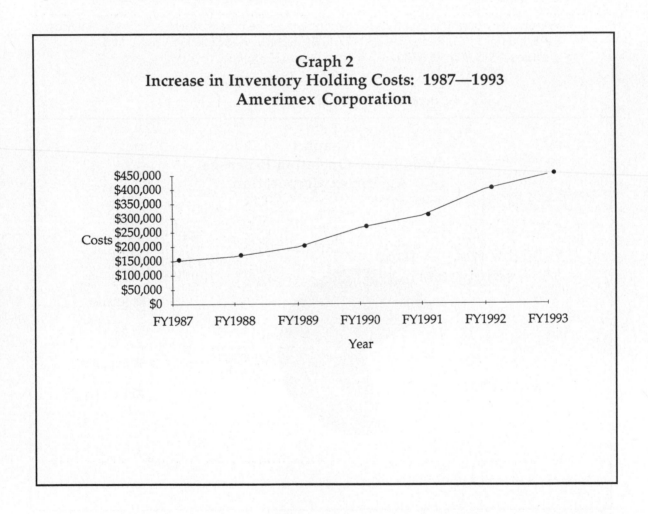

Example 6-4
Line Graph

Bar Graphs

Use bar graphs to compare items or variables, often at different times. Besides giving it a number and a title, you should construct a bar graph following these basic guidelines:

- **Use a zero base.**
- **Use equal intervals on each axis.**
- **Label all parts clearly.**

If you tell your reader that the six industry leaders that adopted JIT "all experienced a substantial decrease in inventory holding costs," you are being vague. If you presented all of the data in paragraph form as in our previous examples, you are being confusing. If you provided both specific data and a graph, you clearly illustrate the comparison of costs before and after adopting the JIT system.

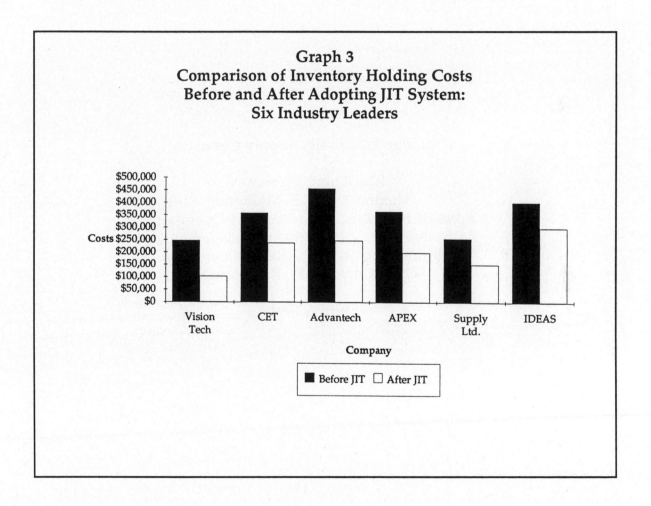

Example 6-5
Bar Graph

Reducing Amerimex Assembly's Inventory Holding Costs through JIT Inventory

Proposal to
Amerimex Assembly

from
Durango Electronics Supply Company

Ivan Hunt, President
Theresa Lee, V.P, Marketing
Edward Simmons, V.P., Overseas Operations
Charles Low, V.P., Software Development
Geraldo Nogales, V.P., Retail Operations
Carol Corral, V.P., Purchasing

July 2, 1994

Example 6-6
Business Proposal

Reducing Amerimex Assembly's
Inventory Holding Costs
Through JIT Inventory

Inventory Holding Costs on the Rise

Durango Electronics Supply Company (DESC) completed a study of Amerimex Assembly's supply ordering system. The data reveal that over $2,700,000 was spent last year on inventory holding costs. These costs reflect rent, maintenance, and repair for warehouse facilities; salaries for warehouse employees and supervisors; equipment and supplies; inventory taxes; opportunity costs; waste; and more. These sources also indicate that Amerimex's holding costs have risen 10 percent each year, while inventories have only increased by 3 percent.

Salaries, rent, supplies and utilities are major expenses in operating Amerimex's warehouse (Graph 1).

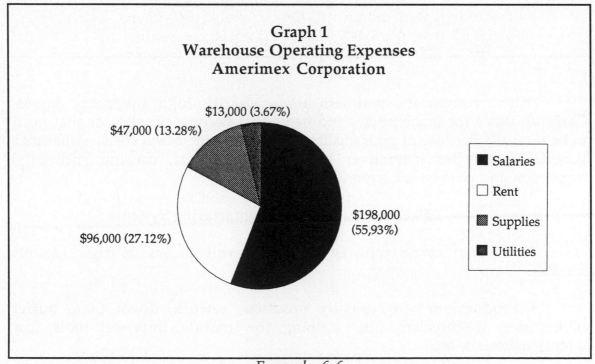

Graph 1
Warehouse Operating Expenses
Amerimex Corporation

$13,000 (3.67%)

$47,000 (13.28%)

$198,000 (55,93%)

$96,000 (27.12%)

- Salaries
- Rent
- Supplies
- Utilities

Example 6-6
Business Proposal

161

Inventory holding costs have increased each year and promise to continue to rise (Graph 2).

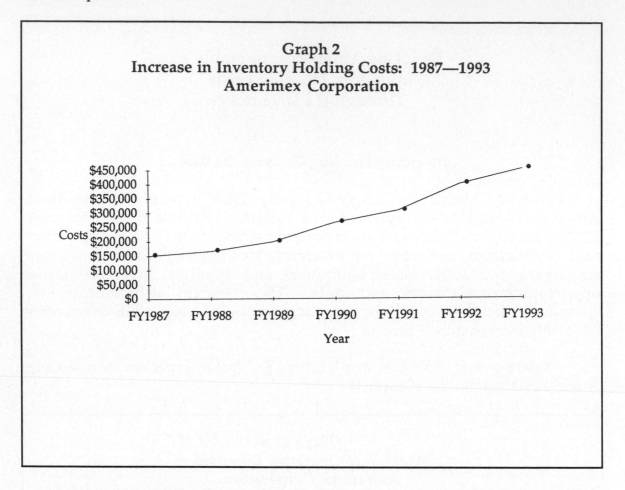

Graph 2
Increase in Inventory Holding Costs: 1987—1993
Amerimex Corporation

Often, companies maintain unnecessarily high inventory levels. Carrying items for emergencies and items that become obsolete or that need to be returned because of poor quality also leads to increased costs. Amerimex purchases supplies from over 100 different outlets, causing additional inspection and paperwork expenses.

Effects of Traditional Manufacturing Systems

Traditional manufacturing systems result in waste from various sources:

• Production: low quality products, rework, down time, buffer inventories, absenteeism, poor training, low morale, improper tools, low quality materials, etc.

Example 6-6
Business Proposal

• Materials: excess materials, obsolete materials, inspection, loss, paperwork, storage, shipping, etc.

• Suppliers: paperwork, too many suppliers, low-quality parts, early or late shipments, returns, sales commissions, poor forecasting, etc.

• Design engineering: poor documentation, poor design, complex design, no testing, late to production, product not targeted correctly, etc.

Strategies for Amerimex

1. Amerimex could continue with its current inventory system.

2. Amerimex could decrease the number of its suppliers, eliminating those with questionable quality standards, developing closer relationships with the remaining companies, and agreeing upon quality standards.

3. Amerimex could implement a "pull" production system, in which individual jobs are completed before supplies for a new job are received; this reduces having to store work-in-process inventories.

4. Amerimex could limit the volume of inventory ordered to that which is needed to complete each project.

Streamline Amerimex's Ordering System

DESC recommends that Amerimex adopt a combination of these strategies in streamlining its ordering system, using a "just-in-time" (JIT) inventory system.

Made successful by the Japanese, JIT was developed in an attempt to reduce inventory holding costs. Several areas of purchasing and manufacturing are affected by JIT. Basically, JIT is a company's campaign to eliminate waste in the manufacturing process.

Characteristics of JIT

Successful implementation of a JIT system involves:

• limiting the suppliers used to those who have shown to be dependable in delivering consistent, zero-defect products.

Example 6-6
Business Proposal

163

- establishing long-term contracts with these suppliers.

- implementing a "pull" production system, ensuring that each job meets quality control standards.

- developing a new ordering policy that meets only current production needs.

Benefits of JIT System

Employing JIT generally brings users three major benefits:

- It reduces inventory holding costs.
- It cuts the number of suppliers, strengthening business relationships.
- It improves product quality.

Implementing a JIT System for Amerimex Assembly

Successful implementation of JIT inventory requires careful, long-range planning and support from all management levels. Major phases of implementing such a program are:

Phase 1: Conceptualizing, Learning and Team Building. Training will take place in an intensive three-month period. The first group of trainees will be hand-picked as those most supportive of the program and most likely to make it succeed. Training will simulate the actual production line process.

Phase 2: Experimenting with Production. Essential to this phase is defining the actual production process. Any changes to the information systems, production line, materials processing, and other manufacturing procedures should be experimented with and observed to "debug" the system. This can be done with just a section of the assembly line.

Phase 3: Implementing the TQC Program. Once the process has been perfected, a Total Quality Control (TQC) program should be implemented. Quality teams must be established to study quality problems and to set quality standards. Training should take place to reach these quality standards. During this phase suppliers who meet the new standards for quality products are identified as those that will be retained.

Example 6-6
Business Proposal

164

Phase 4: Converting to JIT Production. While flexibility is important during this phase, repetitive processing is the norm. Assembly line workers will know their daily goals. They will "pull" supplies only when they need them. The stockroom will send supplies only when they are ordered.

Phase 5: Working with Suppliers. This phase requires patience and convincing the suppliers that JIT is a workable plan. DESC is already eager to work with you on this project.

Phase 6: Evaluating JIT System. Once the JIT system has been fully implemented, it is necessary to evaluate it periodically to determine its effectiveness. Corrections can be made and new goals can be set.

Costs Savings

Amerimex will immediately notice great cost savings. Since you are already connected to DESC's on-line supply network, you will have no initial expenses. Six of the industry's leaders that adopted our JIT program experienced considerable cost savings after the first year (Graph 3).

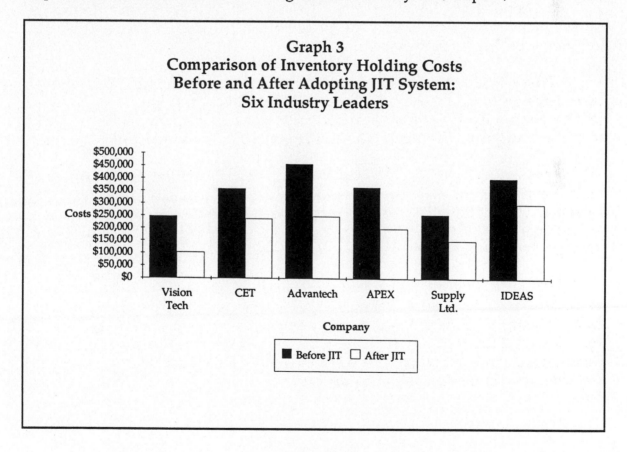

Example 6-6
Business Proposal

165

Amerimex/DESC Agreement

Once you decide to adopt the JIT program, an agreement will be signed. The agreement covers the scope of our relationship, delivery schedules, pricing, billing methods, shipping, warranties, quality agreements, and other contract terms.

You can begin to benefit from JIT today.

Example 6-6
Business Proposal

166

The Oral Presentation

Once you have completed your written proposal, you need to present it to the target audience. You call and make an appointment to meet with the appropriate people.

Purpose Always keep in mind why you are making the presentation. You know that you are there to persuade someone to do something. Remember your one-sentence problem statement, and relate everything to that statement.

Audience Analysis Try to find out as much about your audience as you can. If you can get names, titles, and any other information about who makes up your audience and why they are there, what they already know about your topic, and their attitude toward you and your topic, you can tailor your presentation to fit the situation.

You will also want to determine how you will involve your audience in your presentation. This strategy is frequently overlooked by presenters. If you can involve your audience immediately, you increase the likelihood of a smoother presentation. You can involve your audience through an activity, a questionnaire, or a few questions about your topic. Exercise your creativity here.

Organization Organize your presentation so that you have an effective opening, a logically organized body, and a dominant close.

> **• The Opening** When you open or introduce your presentation, you want to get the attention of your audience. How you do that is your choice; however, a few techniques have worked well for presenters over the years: a startling statement, a rhetorical question, a dramatic story, a personal experience, a quotation from a famous person, a historical event, a reference to a current news story, a quote from *The Bible*, etc.

> **• The Body** The body of your message includes the details of your presentation. You can organize it in various ways, but it should be logical and easy to follow. As with our example, you can organize it using the problem-solution approach. Alternative organizational patterns include compare-contrast, cause-effect, specific to general, general to specific, increasing order of importance, etc.

> **• The Close** Many people do not know how to close a sale; it scares them to ask someone to do something. One way to close your presentation is just like closing a sale; ask your audience to commit to some action. This could be as simple as to read the written proposal and could range to signing a multi-million dollar contract. The most typical close summarizes the presentation or draws conclusions based on the material presented. In any case, end on a dominant note, making it very clear to your audience that you are finished.

> **• The Question and Answer Session** People always want to know more or want clarification on a point, so you should provide time for questions. Your style might dictate that your audience feel free to ask questions throughout your presentation, or you might ask them to hold their questions until you have made your entire presentation. Either way, it is polite to invite questions at the end. You should make a smooth transition between the dominant close and your question-and-answer session.

> You should be able to anticipate most questions; however, some will be new and difficult to answer. If you do not know the answer, say, "I don't know, but I will find out and get back to you." If you are asked questions that have already been covered by your presentation, do not become defensive. Realize that you may need to clarify for some listeners, and that

others in the audience may not have heard everything you said. When you give answers, give complete and honest answers.

Rehearsing your Presentation   Rehearse your proposal presentation. You need to know how long it takes, how well you know your material, where the rough spots are, and how to make smooth transitions between sections and speakers.

Arranging the Room   Arrive early enough to see how the room is arranged. If you are not comfortable with it, make the necessary changes. Test any audio-visual or other equipment to be sure that it works. Make sure that your audience can see your visual aids. Decide whether you should sit, stand, use a podium, etc.

Presenting Your Proposal   Certain practices make for better presentations. Here are some suggestions:

• **Show enthusiasm** . If you look as if you are happy to make your presentation, your audience will be more inclined to listen to you and to believe what you say. A simple "Thank you for allowing me to make this presentation" is a good way to start.

• **Talk to your audience.**   Try to establish a rapport with your audience by talking to each member. Look at each person in the room.

• **Establish eye contact.**   Try to establish eye contact with each member of the audience. Make it direct and brief. Move from person to person. Be sure to turn toward all sides of the audience.

• **Do not read your proposal.**   If you rely too much on your notes or you read your proposal, you will lose your audience. Reading reduces enthusiasm, rapport, and eye contact. It is one of the deadliest things you can do in terms of making a successful presentation.

• **Use voice inflections.**   Voice intonation and inflection sound like normal conversation. You can avoid a monotone by speaking softly, loudly, with raised or lowered endings on words or sentences—just as you talk to a friend.

• **Watch regulators.**   Regulators are "uh," "ah," "you know," and other speaking habits we form to fill in "dead air" time. If you need a second or two to think or refer to a notecard, rather than say "uh-h-h-h," let there be silence. Try to be comfortable with a short period of silence. People will pay less attention to silence than they will to counting the number of times you said "you know."

• **Use gestures appropriately.**   If you make a presentation without any gestures, you run the risk of appearing bored or unenthusiastic, and you may find that you are even more nervous. Some gesturing helps a speaker's nerves. Use your hands to emphasize a point, to illustrate a number (three fingers), and to add life to your verbal presentation.

• **Avoid pacing.**   Try to keep yourself in a small area if you are in front of a large audience. If your style is to move throughout the audience, this may be fine. If you pace back and forth in front of the audience, they may focus more on your pacing than your message.

• **Use humor sparingly.** When novice presenters try to inject jokes into their presentations, they often fail to get the response they intended. Not everyone finds things to be as funny as you see them. Some jokes or stories are inappropriate or lose meaning with the wrong audience. Be very careful. If you have quick wit, you might get just as many laughs with an open, spontaneous remark than with a calculated, canned joke.

• **Manage your time.** When you are given a limited amount of time to make your presentation, stay within it. It is better to run short than to run long. In fact, business people value their time and appreciate meetings that adjourn ahead of schedule. Don't run too short, however, or people might believe you were unprepared and wasting their valuable time.

Assignments:

The Business Proposal

Topic Your company team will write a proposal to another company. Choose a topic that is of interest to one or more of your company's members. Select something that is logical and substantive. You should be creative. Your proposal does not have to deal with anything related to the computer industry or be highly technological in nature. Try to select a subject that will be at least interesting and preferably fun to research and propose. You can propose co-sponsorship of a fund-raiser, a joint venture to build a new children's library for the community, a merger or takeover, etc. The variety of topics is limitless. Use your imagination.

Here is a simple schedule that ensures that every company sends and receives a proposal:

Public Relations Company proposes to Assembly Company
Assembly Company proposes to Manufacturing Company
Manufacturing Company proposes to Retail Company
Retail Company proposes to Supply Company
Supply Company proposes to Software Company
Software Company proposes to Public Relations Company

Content The content and organization of your proposal should follow the model presented at the beginning of this chapter. You should include guide posts or topic headings. and graphics (if appropriate).

Quality As you would with any business document, strive for perfection. Be meticulous about correct grammar, punctuation and spelling. Write for your reader. Be positive. Use an appropriate and attractive format.

Oral Presentation Plan to be responsible for about 20 to 30 minutes. This allows time for your presentation, a question-and-answer period, and feedback from the class. Involve each member of your team in some phase of the oral presentation (introduction, actual proposal, question and answer session, etc.).

Written Presentation Try to create a five-page proposal, including text, graphics, appropriate spacing for emphasis, etc.

169

The Problem Statement

Once your team has a general idea of what you are trying to do with your proposal, you should define your problem in one sentence; for example, "The purpose of our proposal is to persuade the management of Accurex to hire us to conduct a two-day training session on quality circles."

Record your company's problem statement here:

The Proposal Outline

Before you begin to write your proposal, you should always prepare an outline to serve as a tool to help you organize your material. Outlines change as plans change, and you may modify your outline several times before you finish your final document. Write out your initial outline for your proposal here.

Index